Spectral Realms

No. 18 ‡ Winter 2023

Edited by S. T. Joshi

The spectral realms that thou canst see
With eyes veil'd from the world and me.

H. P. LOVECRAFT, "To a Dreamer"

SPECTRAL REALMS is published twice a year by Hippocampus Press,
P.O. Box 641, New York, NY 10156 (www.hippocampuspress.com).
Copyright © 2023 by Hippocampus Press.
All works are copyright © 2023 by their respective authors.
Cover artwork: *Dante and Virgil in Hell* by Filippo di Liagno (called
Filippo Napoletano), 1619–20. Cover design by Dan Sauer.
Hippocampus Press logo by Anastasia Damianakos.

ISBN: 978-1-61498-398-9   ISSN 2333-4215

Contents

Poems

The Star-Treader: Emperor of Dreams

Carl E. Reed

Clark Ashton Smith filled my mind with incredible worlds, impossibly
beautiful cities, and still more fantastic creatures.

—Ray Bradbury

Far-seer of the void & farther realms
illumined by ancient sidereal light,
this wizard of the weird oft overwhelms
one's senses with transfixing eldritch sights.
Incantatory words bright flame & smoke:
opium dreams red-smolder on the page;
though Klarkash-Ton eschewed unhinging dope
his visions proved him sorcerer & mage:
green-mossed statue sunk in Sargasso Sea,
restless ghost adrift in Stygian dark;
white marble temple crumbled to debris,
lost dying ember sun: last hiss & spark.
The Bard of Auburn's verse limns Romantic
Eros, Thanatos, the necromantic.

Fée Metropolitain

M. F. Webb

She is discovering her power, what it means
to be heard. She is ballet and a whisper
which shakes stone, the secret climbing
vein of the city. Her lair: hotel
kitchens, buried stream beds, portals of brick
and water. Stainless steel. Soiled
ribbons. Complex diamonds.

She has moved from primeval
forest to troubled city. You may hear her
in the dying breath of traffic at midnight, the clamor
of knife and fork, calling you to court in
the undergrowth of the current. Even
in this day, some dreams
cast shadows you can follow
with crumbs of yearning.

Pericula Noctis

(Dangers of the Night)

Frank Coffman

Deep in the Night there lurk perils most dire,
Portals gape wide when the pale moon holds sway.
New Moon is worst when no semblance of fire
Keeps out the dark from *Black Stars*–as in day
Cosmic Abysses are kept from our view.
Beings can cross when such gloom hides the tear;
Veil Between Worlds rends and *They* may pass through.
That is the time all Mankind should beware.
Dangers compound for those daring to go
Far from the relative safety of home,
Far from the places and people they know.
Nights become stranger the farther they roam.
Many the reasons to fear well the Night,
For there be *Things* that are far worse than Fright.

The Siren

Carole Abourjeili

The Siren swayed her splendid reign
Bewitched the king to her house of pain
She orchestrated a grand parade
She chained the king to her earthly shade
The king fell deep in her blazing blade.

He quenched her thirst 'the little death'
Thus, gasping through from breath-to-breath
Her mortal cup bled drops of red
Her sinful lust he bred and fed
Yet into her fevered world he lay
The Siren lured him to her prey.

She cut his chords from limb to limb
To craft an instrument on his whim
Her lips thus swayed upon his strings
Her vocal chords began to sing
She rendered her moon with grace-divine
Two bodies, one soul thus did entwine
She summoned his demons to stand and rise
Into her haunted paradise
His demons rose thus adorned her skin
"Beneath your moon I shall lay my sin"

She wore his name her midnight throne
She drowned her depth into his unknown
The enchanted Siren thus wept so deep
Amidst his demons she lay to sleep.

Inspired and written for John William

Banshee

Christian Dickinson

She walked at twilight 'pon the plains of Kowth;
Beside the pillar-stones, and barrows mound.
A child of Éire, native of the south,
Who in the wastelands all her pleasure found.

She from her father's house was wont to roam,
And minded not her mother's warning lay:
"Tread not the plains nigh Rill Boyne in the gloam,
For all that land then longeth to the Fae."

Upon a pillar-stone the young girl stayed,
And 'gan to twine her wayward, carmine hair.
When next the barrow rose a woman's shape;
A wailing cry did prick the child's nape,
And to the cottage did she swift repair,
To find her mother on her deathbed laid.

Front Piece from the Necronomicon

James Arthur Anderson

It remains locked away in a lead-lined vault
far from the prying eyes of probing scholars.
Those few who have seen it say it glows in the dark
in chameleon shades of violet, green, and red.
Its shapes morph like mist, transforming from tentacled things
and piscine faces to hydra heads
and fungi that reek of ageless decay.
The once-human vellum is trimmed with runes
from a language no one has spoken in a thousand years.
It lies interred in its tarnished crypt
and waits for the time when its secrets
will be turned loose once again.

The Ghoul's Delirium

Scott J. Couturier

In this oubliette I endure eternities—
cold, damp concavity of rock sunk beneath
foundations of a mountain fastness.
Cold breathes through stone—I moan
& thrash & scrabble, lean thing of spare
sinew & bone, flesh long-ravaged
by loathsome fungi of subterranean grue.
Yet—a deathless thing am I, though they
knew it not when they cast me into this
accursed hole. A ghoul in fair human guise,
ripe on fatness of mortuary flesh,
able to mingle among mortals at will—
but my marvels incurred a kingly wrath.
Beaten & tortured, deprived of food
(what little bread they brought I could
not stomach; a cellmate I had, my
sole provender in that dread place).
At last, discovering my grisly act, they
threw me (irony!) in this black sepulcher
to starve. Others rotted in pits nearby—
I hurled myself headlong at granite walls
in frenzy until their delicious stench
curdled to mummification's miasma.
That I gnawed at myself I cannot deny—
but no satiation such self-consumption

confers. Kingdoms rise & fall above:
I hear imperious tread of boots on marble,
the impious din of clashing swords.
Sweet blood shed in profusion, but not one
drop leaks to my infernal tomb! I sustain
myself on grotesque larvae that crawl in
through cracks in the floor; their blood is
crude & cold, flesh gelatinous & sour
to my taste, but without them even I—
Deathless—would waste away to ash.

Now, that fortress lies a ruined pile.
I know because no more boots or
horses sound, nor fresh blood stains
those halls long-toppled. Only callow
caw of crows, high & remote, & an
endless scratching of scouring rats.
Yet still I abide in this dark abyss,
awaiting my release—whether by some
unwitting hand or weary weathering
of time & element. What world will I
find at internment's ease? I shudder
to imagine vast feasts of foul meat,
scrabble anew at the one-ton granite plug
inhuming me in this hellish crèche.

I malinger as aeons elapse, flood of
gruesome phantasmagoria my only
sustenance save the pale, porous worm-flesh
which floods up from catacombs obscure,
glut on entrails of Titans I care not to taste
(save vicarious via them)—I fantasize that
these Dead Gods will waken & rend my crypt,
disinterring me to raven once again.
Great maggot-mouthed gods of celestial bloat,
whose limbs drip plagues, whose eyes are
abomination: they would make of all the world
an abattoir. Lonely, decaying, I cry my
plight into their corrupted dreamings,
for my board would never empty in
their kingdom, but only pale, endlessly
erupting grubs testify to their presence.
With a hyena's snout for debilitation
I sense the unseen sun above growing
fat & old: perhaps it will be my sumptuous
lot, at the very end, to devour it.

Pumpkin Ale

K. A. Opperman

An orange potion steeped in pumpkin spice,
Recalling autumns lost, and yet to be,
This rustic ale casts such witchery
Over my soul, my fancy to entice.

This is the kiss of witches candy-sweet,
Like cinnamon on apple-shapen lips. . . .
Beneath a spell, with ever deeper sips,
I grow unsteady on my hay-strown seat.

Now all the owls sing a goblin song,
And bats betide October's chill approach;
Such haunting strains of cricket-chirps encroach
On twilight silence—it will not be long.

It won't be long till autumn hangs her flags
Of gold and crimson in the sighing trees,
And so I drain my flagon to the lees,
And dream of scarecrows, kings in tattered rags.

Trapped in the Spiral Maze

Adele Gardner

Tread with care. The higher you climb, floors collapse,
sagging softly, boards weak with time. My mental
chant supports each step—fragile ice. We night owls
glide across, arms out like wings, seeking midnight
spirits—Dad's mom, walking up here, her black cat
crying, trapped, alone, the wire of death wound tight.

These too-dense layers of memory, wound tight
enough they merge. All our yesterdays collapse
into Now. Grandma sorts treasures, her black cat
frantic, blocking each mouse hole, too much mental
work to stop each scampering thought. By midnight
all the guards are down. Wide night welcomes night owls.

Spiral staircase to nowhere but death: night owls
ring the attic with omen-calls, grief wound tight
through presentiment till noon feels like midnight.
Any time *not* spent with loved ones brings collapse—
guilt, anticipatory grief, a mental
trap, running circles. I must pet my black cat—

Silky smooth, soothing. But it's Grandma's black cat,
who was once ours. She changed us into night owls,
flying around her back garden—a mental
war game, Grandma said, for when the world wound tight,
a noose—reality ready to collapse

our airways. Pet cats. Be asleep by midnight.
In some parts of my heart, it's always midnight.
The only cure I ever found: my black cat,
on my chest, purring: heaven. Can I collapse
that in a vial? An antidote for night owls
whose anxiety keeps their dreams locked, wound tight
with dread, perfect prison, because it's mental?

Anxiety spiral or haunting? Mental
torture chamber of memories gone bad: a midnight
that never ends. Dream visitors trapped, wound tight
in my grief. Floors break: falling. Basement black cat
helps Dad in his workshop cook up new night owls,
their hoots lifting hearts, fending off world's collapse.

All magic's mental, so you need a black cat
to guide you home at midnight. Clever night owls
bind your lost soul's wound, tight enough to collapse.

Brain Funk

Maxwell I. Gold

Never were there conditions so dark, so damp, but those pits depressed my mind. Deep, deranged, and quite burdensome, they were riddled with such a stink, where my thoughts were twisted into submission. The cyber gods of funk pressed harder, their foulness almost as real as my dreams, staining this place with the abhorrence of sweet rot and dread; the wild cosmic stinkhorn rooted within a curdled, blasted rhizome. Still, onward I walked inside that most terrible of places, a darkness like no other, under a black palace constructed long ago by my wretched imagination. Tall, jagged ramparts stretched high into the foggy, gray uselessness of the swampy night. Veiny towers that clogged my memory like hollowed-out dream-castles, emblematic of my self-destruction crumbled under diseased scar-tissue where my sojourned consciousness sought refuge with a few lonely neurons.

What a place, poisoned by the brine of salted corpses that once may have dreams, or perhaps something more beautiful. Now, piled high toward the crooked night, their bodies reeked of my indecision, an aromatic hallucination so thick, the fog throttled my screams.
My body,
    my dreams,
        thousands of them.
I lost count after each endless night as the conditions grew darker, until the cyber gods of funk pressed harder, without a care when soon, nothing remained of my shattered skull.

Aspis; or, The Brood of Rahab

Harris Coverley

If I am pressed, I would say that my kind have always lived since the Beginning, deep down in the bowels of Tehom, until we rose above the pillars of the Earth, on the fountains of the deep, into the wider seas across from the lands of man and beast. I rise and fall with the seasons, somnolent on the ocean's floor, within the cracks of the crust, until, stirred by an inner rumbling, I float as gently as jetsam to the surface of the waves, greater than the greatest whales who scorn me (*pitiable cretins!*), baring my hide; my grey limbs wide and flat and obscure; my million tendrils as fine as the heather of a fair and hospitable isle, spreading on the air from their many nodes a most seductive sweetness; and I await men foolish enough to try to settle. Yes, one's back is sometimes burned by a sailor's errant fire, but it is a small price for the tired souls of those hopeful for a rest; and when they do lack the sense of wiser folk and bed themselves down for the night amongst the crags of my back, it is so easy to simply sink, sink, *sink*, into the familiar depths, turn up my jaws and feast—O *Great Poseidon!* I pray you avert your holy eyes, and yet allow me the most calamitously arrogant and thoughtless seafarers who have displeased your power! I claim no godhood for myself, only to be your loyal servant . . . give me your grace, give me your courage, give me your strength, O *Lord of this Realm!* I sit a mere fleck within this infinitely dark cerulean plane, and wait . . . and wait . . . soon the next repast . . .

Sisyphus Looks Up

Geoffrey Reiter

He strains beneath the crush of igneous load,
His sinews taut, caught teetering on the shaft
Of that pale peak. The king who late had laughed
At signs and laws divine—the man who sowed
Discord and poured his pride in all that flowed
From out his lips—must now forgo his craft
And cunning, draw the wafting draught
Of death on death, the doom that now he's owed.

The balance shifts, the boulder rolls, the fool
Begins the backward plunge again; yet while
He falls, his eyes behold the blinding darkness
And voids of space, the gulping gulfs that drool
Thick drips of slimy chaos—and his trial
Resumes again beneath the hollow starkness.

The Rite of Exploration

Holly Day

You make me want to drill holes in my skull
wrap wires around my brain, sink drill bits and fingertips into
my body, map the lace of fine blood vessels
with radioactive dyes, trace my skeleton through my skin
with melted solder and #2 pencils
dig a place inside me for you to curl up and sleep
never leave. I want you to have it all:

my skin to wrap in a sheet around your shoulders
or around your waist when you step out of the bath
my skull and pelvis to prop open the door
when you need to bring new furniture into the house
fingers and toes to shim under wobbly table legs and chairs
the rest of my blood to stain the floor more evenly
to match the spot on the wood where I fell.

Dreamsign

Andrew White

(After Stephanie Law's painting; see also "Hummingbirds"
by Yoku Shinizu.)

How do you know that a dream is just a dream?
Life, at times, can seem so surreal,
How to be sure that reality is real?
Where does one end and the other begin—
Follow the signs that rise from within.

Take note of the odd, the strange, the uncanny:
The sight of a mask where it should not be
And a bloody red ribbon, flying free.
Are you hearing sounds you've never heard?
Why does a glow surround that bird?

Dreams can invade your waking hours:
Nightbirds dance in the morning light,
Hummingbirds flock in unnatural flight.
What are the signs that dream is now real?
You can't know for sure, it's something you feel.

Postmortem

Ngo Binh Anh Khoa

Long have my breaths been sealed by Death; my mind,
Though, is still forced to dream within this deep
Void that my coffin opens to. The sleep
Eternal promised to me is denied
Through ages spent trapped in flesh long decayed;
My flickering sentience, like a wind-whipped ember,
Is marred by nightmares—each one I remember
So starkly, for the pains felt shall not fade.
Now, in my latest dream, chained to a table,
I have my vision robbed, my limbs gone numb,
Then from around me, squelching noises come
Till I'm gnawed on by slimy things, unable
To scream with my throat torn or fight their touch.
No peace shall grace my sin-stained soul, and such
Is my damned fate when caught in Death's fell clutch.

Transmogrification

Manuel Pérez-Campos

Protected by concentric rings of cosmic dust,
Jupiter's equinoctial bands look like ribbons
of brown and chartreuse seaweed in distress:

it is within the supersonic soundscape of that
intranquil colossus that drowsy unreal numbers
wake in voluminous dimness and perform

unprecedented operations: I aspire to reincarnate
as a free-floating form of diaphane in the shifting
terra nullius of its interior, that super-kingdom

of permanently loosened moorings, spared the tenseness
that comes from being of my own kind abominator:
it will be like entering a lucid dream that can be reached

only from another lucid dream: fluctuant magneto-
fluorescent chasms shall roar pell mell past me:
I shall be apprenticed to its gale elementals—and

stripped of my attributes until I am unrecognizable
even to myself: and capable of having an unbroken line
of thought of infinite complexity which lasts aeons.

Appalling

Lori R. Lopez

In the town of Appalling, a few clicks past
the edge of Nowhere, smack on the brink
of Madness, we do things differently. Macabre,
you might say. Beyond the pale. At our own
pace, neither fast nor slow . . . We don't even
have such lanes, and nobody carpools unless
they're riding in an Ambulance or Hearse.
The sole traffic light is on the blink. The single
stop sign was crossed out to read GO, a warning:
Turn straight around and go away! As if that's
even possible. (It isn't, it's an oxymoron.)

We from Appalling lack a sense of humor.

Not that we have no Funnybones . . . that would
be anatomically incorrect. We're not all weird!
Folks here just don't find very much amusing,
although we do enjoy a good practical joke,
the crueler (and more practical) the better.
We simply don't laugh. We take our work in
the Death Biz seriously. It requires a degree
of solemnity. (Not a college degree, the other
kind.) I'm a twelfth-generation pallbearer.
My neighbors are undertakers: morticians,
embalmers, and beauticians who doll up
the deceased.

Most of my Appalling friends are diggers
and coffinmakers. A few sell caskets
or plots door to door. Three sisters
run a fancy boutique with tiny dark suits,
little black dresses. My spouse, a cakemaker
and wake caterer, peddles gravemarkers and
life-termination policies on the side.
We met at a funeral directed by Aunt Palline,
who films death scenes too. Our son sculpts
those angels you see in cemeteries. A daughter's
compiling a sequel to her coffee-table tome
on tombstone rubbings.

Not everyone here has morbid tastes. I arrange
flowers and wreaths as a hobby. My mother
paints portraits. (Corpses are the best models!)
There is no law of the land, and hence
no need for enforcement. Residents share
an esprit de corps; the creed of memento mori,
existing by a common code of *Live while you
can because things are bound to get worse!*
Each quickly discovering since birth that

everything around us is appalling.
If you think it sounds bleak . . .

You haven't been to Underwhelming.

There is no such place. But if you really
want to visit, hang a left at the railroad tracks,
drive thirteen miles—watching for trains—
until you come to a dry creekbed. Now you're
as lost as the rest of us! I'm not sure how
to get there because it doesn't exist.
If it did I would tell you. We're not crazy
about tourists in Appalling. Now and then
someone ships their body here to be buried,
since we have so many Graveyards, thinking
we're as restful as the infamous Sleepy Hollow.
We mail them back: RETURN TO SENDER.

(I bet they're still circulating, or stacked in some postal
warehouse for Eternity . . . one of our wicked practical jokes.
You don't want to get us started!)

Stranded in Mississippi

Chad Hensley

On a sweaty summer night, I stroll
A pockmarked stretch of Highway 90,
Dodging pot holes and a dead possum,
The heady scent of fresh cut grass and wild onions
Lingering still.

Magnolias sprawl skyward,
Not really happy with the remnants of revenants in their soil,
Limbs scoliotic and cataracted,
Unable to decide which way
To reach for a heaven
That's surely hidden somewhere just above the domed slate of darkness.

Stooped by the roadside
An old black man, shoeless and skeletal,
Collects desiccated teeth of Civil War soldiers.
Pushes bits of bone into his cavernous gums for an enduring smile.
He'll walk bounteous miles to the French Quarter,
Give his Cheshire grinning as a gift to the Chicken Man
For a voodoo ritual in Lafayette cemetery
Sure to speckle his robin egg eyes for a hundred more years
With rumblings beneath venerable earth and
Antediluvian voices that still remember forgotten festivals of jubilant days.

Over the cooling pavement
Rusting pickup trucks roar

Like runaway trains in heat,
Back windshields covered
With stickers of Confederate flags and fish symbols.
Inside filthy cramped cab darkness,
A mass of bloodshot eyes glows maniacal.
Clawed hands darting toward the gun rack
At the slightest sound of honking.

Throat parched for companionship,
I stop at the Super Walmart,
Looking for a Dixie peach in pigtails and cut-offs.
I find obese zombies shuffling through the aisles on electric carts,
Flabby skin flaps sloughing off in great oily folds,
Fresh dead sea scrolls for future generations.

In an adjacent pasture
Decapitated clansmen whistle for their bodies,
Ghostly white hoods whirling in the wind like discarded laundry,
Trails of rising steam.

Back on the tarmac,
All I've got to show for my travels
Is a dime bag of Mexican dirt weed and a pocket full of change,
Hoping for high plains drifter,
A mockingbird's song somewhere in the distance ahead of me.

Dreams of the Styx

Steve Dilks

Sit with me upon the ground (said he);
I have so much to tell;
Over there in the trees black shade
Are where the wild kings fell.
Sit with me here upon the shore;
And listen to the wild winds sing
Listen to the strains of a golden harp
That whispers at half grasped dreams.
Gaze with me now across the night;
To where the sunset gleams with red
Up to where the moons rise with pallid light
And kingdoms are forgotten as the dead.
Dream with me of the sphinx's black mask
Gaze on where the old dynasties sleep;
Where eternity rests in a golden cask;
Between her claws where the shadows creep.

I turned to the sound of a sweeping oar,
And saw lined against the marbled moon
A long black boat pull into shore
And knew a peculiar doom.
At the tiller a spectral hand;
A shrouded figure dressed in black;
Beckoning to the sunset land—
the resting land where none comes back.

He spoke a word with a spectral groan;
My friend brushed past me as one in thrall
As I went to hold him his broken blade slapped my chest; 'Mine is the
life that must atone.'
He stalked in tattered armour to the shore's bleak edge
and the figure greeted him there
If not frozen I would have fled—
From beneath that hooded figure's solemn stare.
A mist fell before my eyes
Somewhere a harp played a bitter song
and on weeping, dreaming tides
The boat fared forth and then was gone.

There upon the edge of waters black
I stood and gazed out across the night
With crystalline towers rising through the mist
beneath the moons pallid light.
I saw him then in ghostly pall
As the boat sailed onto waters black
And into the misted silent falls
They sailed to the land where none comes back.

I awoke in the light of a pale grey dawn
On the dirty river's misty side
I lifted my gaze to the somber morn

From the mire of the sluggish tide
I saw no purple towers rising there
Rearing through an elusive mist
I saw only a shabby town
And memories of a friend now missed
I groped for the half-empty bottle near my hand
To wipe the pain of life away
And dreamed of a river wider than land
At the sunset remains of day.

Ghosts in Their Sunday Clothes

Steven Withrow

Ghosts in their Sunday clothes are leaving town
As more arrive in homespun every week.
The dress of death is always trending down.

The woman in white, of late, is wearing brown;
The suicide's ensemble's now antique.
Ghosts in their Sunday clothes are leaving town.

The long-dead heiress sells her sleekest gown
To a legless phantom void of all mystique.
The dress of death is always trending down.

Even the graveyard king, who found his crown
When he lost his head, is fleeing with the chic.
Ghosts in their Sunday clothes are leaving town,

And their keening's nearly loud enough to drown
The low hiss of the living, so to speak.
The dress of death is always trending down.

Though fashion snobs might meet it with a frown,
The local situation's not unique:
Yes, ghosts in their Sunday clothes are leaving town,
But the dress of death is *always* trending down.

The Spirit Mirror of Doctor Dee

Ann K. Schwader

A foreign disk of midnight glass,
it whispers in its master's hands
with tongues of spirits—or of gods—
eradicated from their lands

& craving vengeance. His dread queen
who seeks to cleanse the seas of Spain
is now their weapon, though she knows
no portion of this. In a reign

so perilous, she cannot spare
too much concern for hows or whys:
whatever Dee's *black stone* may be,
she blinks & lets the compromise

hang mute between them. He, in turn,
must prove himself a thing of use
beyond replacement—wizards fail
but once (the royal hangman's noose

if fortunate). He stakes his fate
on stars & portents understood
by few who scry the forward arc
of history: a brotherhood

Hermetic, esoteric . . . blind
to pagan underworlds that gape
behind reflections. Dee alone
has glimpsed the Mictlan, tracing shapes

of Aztec nightmare. Prophecy
speaks strangely here. These ancient dead
viewed through obsidian appear
as starving shadows, to be fed

or sulk in silence. Shuddering,
he makes his bow & takes his leave,
retreating to his study where
a blade awaits. Beneath his sleeve

a palimpsest of scars betrays
the cost of knowledge to such cursed
& gifted men. His mirror moans—
he cuts again, to slake its thirst.

The Old Ones: A Ghazal

Joshua Gage

The earth was birthed, and nameless beings came for the old gods,
rapacious creatures from primordial mire that flamed for the old gods.

The scratch of straw pokes between the padding of her cell.
She claws the walls and shrieks, her mind insane for the old gods.

Penumbral planets whirl across the spectral maw of the cosmos,
jagged, rock-strewn husks of temples profaned for the old gods.

From out the tempest, blades of lightning stab the emerald waves
and rend the waters wide of fill with flames for the old gods.

Echoes of the starless sky choke the fetid sea.
On the harbor lighthouse writing your name for the old gods.

A yellowed tooth. A vial filled with blood. A pinky finger.
Acolytes, exalt your bodies maimed for the old gods.

Among the droops of monkshood, the glare of yellow eyes by moonlight.
A Romani violin shrieks refrains for the old gods.

The high priest intones forgotten rites to summon unbodied shadows.
With spectral hands, they mark his head ordained for the old gods.

Eons of dust have settled on the anthropodermic tome.
Its words contort your mind into a domain for the old gods.

Rank with sweat and vomit, the sacrifices scratch their bonds.
Every orifice is ripe terrain for the old gods.

Will you let the rampant thorns cicatrix your skin
in arboraceous penance, again and again, for the old gods?

Chiseled hieroglyphics shudder and drip with ebon ichor.
Drink down this communion we maintain for the old gods.

Take up your blades and prowl the world until the cosmos swells
With echoing keens of heretics slain for the old gods.

A thousand smokes defile the air as fevered prayers crescendo.
Frothing novitiates shake their chains for the old gods.

Grandma's fragile reliquary begins to shake and steam
into plumes of putrid clouds gathering rain for the old gods.

Cobwebs of cable span the river where the rabble baptize
themselves in rancid waste, a flock sustained for the old gods.

Glazed with skeletal moonlight, our fermented minds repine.
All lucid sense and acumen wane for the old gods.

She snarls through the library, gnawing at the pages
willingly dedicating her book-fevered brain for the old gods.

Verdant aisles of sylvan night hide eternal fears.
Follow the songs to the marble altar, blood-stained for the old gods.

Belfries buckle against the eclipse, incessantly tolling alarms.
Revelers wander the streets, drunk on champagne for the old gods.
Moldy candlelight dances the ossuary walls
inumbrating the olid bones we became for the old gods.

Vultures descend to taste his tears as he sobs in the throes of anguish.
The flap of their wings harmonizes with his pain for the old gods.

Pestilential vapors reek across the xanthous swamp
where fervent mothers drown their newborns, claimed by the old gods.

Gape your lips to nocturnal pus that squirms from out the stars
then execrate this land with mantras exclaimed for the old gods.

The seas have receded, and now the Pilgrim slithers from ruin to ruin.
Salt-stained, barnacled timbers are all that remain for the old gods.

For Those Who Tread the Narrow Path

Jordan Zuniga

Not all who endure in the shadows
Are abandoned by the hope of the light,
Not all who walk in the darkness
Are without a means of sight,
Not all who trail the long road
Are without a destination in the mass,
Not all who choose the sting in the shadows
Are unable to believe it will pass,
Not all who linger in the pit
Are without a hope to conceive,
Not all who choose to wait
Are without anything to believe,
Not all who endure what seems so strange
Are weird for enduring the spectre, the wraith,
Not all who gain the thorn of affliction
Are without the strongest of faith.

In the Land of Magma, Salt, and Glacier

Amelia Gorman

In the land of magma, salt, and glacier
Teetering waypoints mark the older roads.
Gray rock-on-rock pyramids defy wind.
Defy all forces except erasure
By human hands seeking to change the map.

And just like that the sign is a trap
That should have marked the turn to a nice
Farmhouse selling yoghurt or a waffle
Peaked with homemade cream and a scarlet cap
Of crowberry jam. Where you meant to turn.

Some trickster has sent you away to burn.
Some sorcerer's hand restacked the standing
Stones so instead of safety, a doorway
Appears to a land-in-a-land. A fern
Drenched caldera gaping straight to hell.

Where scarlet demons play and ill winds swell.
Your breath shatters the air with each exhale.
Smoke rises from the chimneys underground,
Dead roots grab your feet. It is no church bell
That peels from the peeked white steeple. It calls

The dead from graves from mines from hungry halls,
Where cold fire burns in the common room.
It's a wooden whale sounding in the dark.
The poems of Egil, the burning of Njal's
Family. Older roads opening up.

There is no warmth here, but there is a cup
You take from the dead, no farmhouse coffee.
The first time since your arrival something
Burns. Hungry, you have no choice but to sup
With these corpses, from their silver and lore.

You eat with remains of thingmen tossed ashore
By winter winds like a stick of driftwood.
You break bread with murderers and outlaws,
Slurp the fat of lamb, gelatinous hoar
Congealing on the meat and dripping sin.

The sparse landscape reveals the burnt feast within
Beneath the ridge, there are platters peak-high.
Stolen cheese from starving neighbors, thieves' eyes
Severed by a tooth. Warm as your own skin
The meal opens itself and you partake.

Like your guts turn west and not east. Skies break
Against the craters. You can't go home, but
You can eat at this birch table, you can
Raise glasses with these bones, you can make
A meal here with the dead, below this glacier.

Giants in the Earth

Darrell Schweitzer

The Bible says there were giants in the earth in those days.
It's true.
There still are,
only they're much older than the Bible or mankind.
Sometimes you can see their shapes
in the contours of the hills,
in the bare stone faces of cliffs,
particularly at sunset or in shadow:
swarming schools of monsters,
sounding and breaching like whales
 amid million-year dreams
in which a hundred centuries is as a second,
and their slightest turnings or sighs
are only measurable in geological time.

Pray that they remain so:
If they should ever awaken,
they will surely brush us away
like vermin off a dirty bedsheet.
Pray that their sleep is long.

The Song of the Sword

Adam Bolivar

The Song of the Sword   is sorrowful to hear:
Fate-forged,   fear-bringer,
Hero-held,   hilt graven with
Runes of ruin,   wrack of giants,
Thirsty thorn   threatening doom,
Who holds its hilt   hears the song,
Woden's wail,   the woe of gods,
Fallen, faded,   feared no longer.
The sword still   slays their foes,
Blade black   with blood spilled
On ravening runes,   restless to feast,
And give the gods   a ghostly joy.

Night Comes to Sesqua Valley

D. L. Myers

For WHP

In Sesqua Town, the silent shadows creep
And with the setting sun great Selta's shroud
Unfurls upon the silver-eyed unbowed
By night's eternal spells of mist and sleep.
The forest paths all glow with subtle light
And stealthy figures tread the spreading dark
In search of Moonlight's grim and argent spark
To pierce the black, unfathomed pool of night.

And through the haunted woodland's heart, they go
Dark pilgrims on a cryptic quest to find
That vague and starlit, darksome way defined
By Dreamland's fey and misty, eldritch glow.
So, hand in hand, the Children pass beyond
To live the dream that darkest Night has spawned.

Herod Agrippa

Acts 12:21–23

Wade German

False god enthroned, the monarch sits
Surrounded by his sycophants.
They praise his words as honey-writ;
To minion and to hierophant,
His palace seems a sacred shrine
For they have deemed their king divine.

But now his brain aches; now, it burns . . .
How could a *god* feel so unwell?
He quivers, and his stomach churns;
Have witches placed on him a spell?
Or had he something foul to eat—
Has poison touched the man-god's meat?

His minions flee, the high-priest wails:
They see black blisters on his skin!
Agrippa, now in seizure, flails,
Howling that something gnaws within!
His flesh is rotted-green and squirms—
And bursting forth . . . are worms, are worms!

Corvid Hill

David Barker

Uncounted years below the hill had sprawled
A rustic town where simple folk had dwelt.
From jagged cliffs above black ravens called,
Haranguing those below, or so they felt.
Some spoke of sending men up there with knives
To slash the throats of those offensive birds,
But wiser folk warned "Do not risk your lives!
The hill avenges such, you mark our words!"

That very night, their sleep disturbed by screams,
A fall of bloodied feathers raining down.
All saw the ravens murdered in their dreams
By men with blades who climbed up from the town.
And then the town was *gone*, no trace was left –
And laughter rumbled from the highest cleft!

Inspired by H. P. Lovecraft's sonnet "VII. Zaman's Hill" in *Fungi from Yuggoth*

Visiting Hours

John Thomas Allen

I will write you in the dream ministry
and the yellow ledger it has on
each bit of fractal magic passed
from the apple of Adam's eye, now sleeping.
These porch skeletons and the flowers
they hatch on your deserted moon villa,
on the song whispered in a siren's tune,
the kindle of an Arabian fire and the phantasy light
sleeping on the church lawns.
I will unfurl Aladdin's blanket,
hand on the sundial's IV
waiting the time you attend,
in the green lit skulls rising
in the drumroll ministries
in the drop hour by hour.
in this half chill, this moon faced haunting.
And this is where hours of visitation grow
a perfumed blade of the uncouth,
the voodoo penicillin wrapped in tags
around your neck. And this is where
our hours of visitation grow
a perfumed blade of the uncouth,
tags in druidic longhand. Arnim's

blue spider bites, and in its web
I sink, I struggle, your hands warm
with headdresses of incense,
and this noir haunting for which you
went so far beneath the ground.

In Your Dreams

Silvatiicus Riddle

Go on, then—
pull me from your dream.

Perched like a devil on the sill, I watch
spirit return to form and sinew and sweat,
clothed by shadow and soft tongues of silk,
lapping at the tender flesh like shallow plates
of cardamom and honey-milk.

Damned to the mutable field of memory,
forever a stranger in the undiscovered country
'tween sleep and awake;
I crave you in this, my short and fleeting life
as surely as your body craves me.
Like the cursed woman,
your soft, shallow breaths
between aching breasts alone
could mark you with heresy.
The gird and thrust of your hips—
a veritable study in demonology.

Could I taste the bitter pomegranates of your mouth?
Could we tarry beneath the rowan trees
till the rain carries us as dust to the river,
filling our tattered pockets with fishes and loam?

Could I keep you in a ceaseless now,
swaddled like a babe
in tender robes of dew and starlight?

Somehow man and somehow beast,
yet I weigh not more than a sigh
hanging softly on tepid summer air;
am I all that you ever wanted,
the apotheosis of your greatest desire?
Are you broken by the curse of waking?
And I, by the laws
that our hands, fistfuls of darkness, may never meet,
our souls never touch?

I become nothing:
a ripple on the curtain's sway,
mist upon the flowers
pierced by morning light.

Post-anthropy

David C. Kopaska-Merkel

The soup is cold, she spoons it from the can,
Outside the window nothing moves at all,
Come morning she'll be foraging again,
In kitchens, supermarkets, eateries.
Carefully she steps among the bones,
Of women, men, and children, pets and rats,
She's got no clue why she alone was spared,
But it's been months and food is running out.

Beyond Manhattan are there people liv-
ing? Birds or squirrels at least for company?
Or is Lord Death the undisputed King,
From sea to stinking lifeless plastic sea?
Last woman on the island dreams of love,
Her mother's arms, her father's stubbled cheek.

Mr. Illusive

Frank Coffman

Time has flown since a century and a half ago
A heinous killer prowled East London's paths;
A villain whose name we'll likely never know
Left in his wake horrific aftermaths:
Multiple murders, mutilations grim,
Disfigurements, disembowelings dire—
Yet he was never caught! No proof of him
Who, no doubt now, burns in Hell's hottest fire.

Working for one more gin or one night's doss,
Enduring shame for a tiny pittance earned,
Not knowing just how great would be their loss,
Their suffering, their final lesson learned:
Tabrum? perhaps, then Nichols, Chapman, Stride
All walked the East End streets—and there they died.
The last—it seems? Mary Kelly lost her life
In Miller's Court, cruelly carved by this monster's knife.

Unfortunately, police work in those times,
Was woefully unprepared to solve these crimes.
Oh, there were suspects—many!—were *and are,*
But no investigation has gone very far.
A cryptic message in chalk quick washed away,
A package with gory kidney wrapped within;
Suspects abound, yet—elusive to this day—
Just who was guilty of this trail of sin.

But a letter, likely fake, writ in blood red

(Of its lack of provenance most are quite sure),
It's rambling message generally unknown—Instead
It is well-remembered for its signature:
"I want to get to work right away . . . good luck.
Yours Truly Jack the Ripper." That has stuck.

The Venomous Violins

Ron L. Johnson II

The Violins dissolve your tissue like sulfuric acid.
The hemotoxic venom is not placid.
In the nocturnal, the tiny Violins can't be seen;
The Violins view you with their six-eye-gleam.
In the day the Brown Violins seem absent,
Yet, between the walls, omnipresent.

Don't ever close your eyes or they can seize
Because all their eyes are opened wide
While your eyes only see dreadful dreams.
If you have been bitten in the face with their toxic trace
Their venom is worse than being sprayed with mace.

If the tiny eight spindly legs scurry across your floor
Your exit may be nocturnally obstructed until the sun rises more.
Sometimes, after the Violin's fangs inject their toxic gore,
A furious fever can intensely ensue;
Or perhaps you're one of the unlucky few
And the Venomous Violins cause your demise
Before anyone else even knew.

A Whisper to Rock

Carl E. Reed

My poetry is like
the final exhalation
of the broken-limbed body
that plunged into a pit
fell a hundred feet
hit bottom
& bounced.

The shock of impact:
like the slap of a colossus with hands of granite—
the crushing weight of a tank
grinding a soldier into gore—
a thousand-ton standing stone
toppling onto a wide-eyed
writhing victim.

What matters
is the pain.

What counts
is the effacement
of all personality & thought
by agony:
a bolt of thunder-flame
wielded by dwarven wizards
warring in a dark caldera—

a towering wave
from the Sargasso Sea
breaking against boulders
left stranded & forlorn
on the distant shore
of some alien & desolate land
by the passage of glaciers ancient
powerful, & doomed
as vanished
Neanderthal nations.

After crash & boom
of the black wave—
frothing foam in the backwash
skirling across crab-scuttled sands.

:::*whisperwhisper*:::
last faint words
muttered to the rock
pressed against my lips.

In Tura

Scott J. Couturier

Just outside Cairo in forgotten Tura,
where pharaoh's limestone was mined:
primordia for Khufu's Great Pyramid,
prized for funereal frieze & palace graving,
vast white blocks hewn out & honed
from caverns deep as desert's malice,
all eld Egypt built up from your bones.
The most sacred temple's enclosure boasts
that white limestone of Tura: lavish tombs
lie heavy with long-ago freighted slabs,
delved in ancient epoch by ghosts who
anonymous knew immortality of their
worldly works. Incised by unnumbered
hieroglyphs, divine & mundane: cast as
stela & sarcophagi, mastaba & monument,
revered even in godhood's guise! How many
untold years & lives poured out over your
pale, pliant stone? Tura: now home solely
to dust & loneliness, no more to build
up bastions of Ra's earthly eminence,
unwrought, remaining in wait for some
future age when your rock is again
needed, your silence filled with hammer
& chisel's wrack, & ageless workers' songs.
But now, your forsaken quarries house

wanderers seeking shelter from the sand:
niches abandoned by Time & labor
frozen & scoured down with gradualness
of eternity, with patience of grain & wind.

Figments and Fragments

William Clunie

Paralyzed in this bleak world
I walk in nighttime realms
and awaken to a face that hangs
upon a melting wall, a mouth
that whispers tales of the bric-a-brac
of dreams. Such mornings it takes time
to shed the ominous fantastic
of the nightmare hours; I think
I age a year in every night
but some of those gray horrors
disappear by light of day,
a recollection of those terrors
as jejune, idols of ancient
acolytes, white wimples fading
over the horizon, rebel angels
that claim an outcast race: nothing
fantastic about the night, I remind
myself; the past is prose, the future,
fragments of inelegant poems.

From Heights of Fire to Depths of Cold

Andrew White

(After the movie *Touched with Fire*)

Eyes that burn with silver fire,
A body that simply will not tire,
Reaching out for something higher—
Looking to the moon above

A mind beset by scorching stones
Till frostbite settles in her bones,
A labyrinth of black unknowns—
Staring through the cosmic void

Silent storms in cold abyss
Scaly things that feed on bliss
Something truly is amiss—
Searching for another world

Rollin' Bone and Beaten Stones

Harris Coverley

I drove up to the pump
and the skeleton who ran the place quavered on out from his hut

his hoary yellow boiler suit clung to his bones as did once his flesh
his eyes blue marbles sown into the sockets for the pretence
his default grin reminded me of a frozen waterfall
its individual streams entombed in porcelain white threads

"fill her up," I said not smiling back
and he released the pump
filled with the blood of many less fortunate travellers
and jammed it into my '67 Mustang

I wandered off
considered a burger from the snack bar
the kiosk carved from the kneecap of a banished god
but I could not spare the coins from my eyes

past those coppers
I glanced at the sun
purple and throbbing
fracturing into three or so chunks of bad energy

***

I looked down the road
and saw only grey sand
and the black vein of cracking tarmac
stretching into the Nothing
of an inconceivable horizon
of colours not seen by mortal men

the attendant called me back over
and I tore off the little finger
from my left hand
and paid him with it

he gave me my receipt
and then asked, "d'ya have anythin' left to say?"

"what?" I replied like the fool I am

"anythin' left to say, *before* . . . ?"

I thought about it for a moment
then I wrote down some final words on the back of the receipt

I handed him the slip of paper
"keep 'em—they're yours"

*   *   *

and I jumped into the Ford
slammed on my Beefheart tape
and rolled off
and onwards to Oblivion.

The Troublemaker; or, To Escape Days of Idleness

Manuel Pérez-Campos

This armchair, this pipe, these slippers,
and Baroness Orczy's book, fit my discordial mood;
Gaelic liquor, too: and this fiery hearth to help me brood.
Give me a treasure map, and moths in my purse,
and I will outwit the King's armies, curse
the Angels, and with society's Grand Ladies
be masterfully rude; dogs will nip at my heel,
mobs and appletrees will yearn for my neck.
Straight from Oberon, after a cards' deal,
my bagpipe melodies will on death's sleep intrude
and raise the Kraaken to the Captain's deck.
Mephistopheles will kneel, redeemed; encyclopedias
will print blank pages; Tristan's certitude
will be mine--and Isolde will laugh along, and tease.

.

The Dragon's Rage

Ngo Binh Anh Khoa

(A Vietnamese *lục bát*)

What goes up must come down;
What goes round must come round once more—
This Karmic Law of yore
Was set and evermore shall stay.
All deeds done shall one day
Be judged and squared as they deserve.

Good deeds good karma serve
While evil deeds reserve ill things.
Yet, Man to evil clings,
Whose greed-fueled actions bring much pain
To all across the plane,
Chained to this selfish reign they've wrought.

Lục bát (six–eight) is a traditional Vietnamese poetic form that alternates
between a six-syllable line and an eight-syllable line. Lục bát poems vary in
length, with the shortest having exactly two lines, commonly seen in folk poetry.
The rules of lục bát are strict and complex because of six tones that are integral
to the Vietnamese language, but in English these tones do not exist, so the
rhyming rules are less complicated. Simply put, a lục bát poem opens with a six-
syllable line, whose final syllable must rhyme with the sixth syllable of the eight-
syllable line. The final syllable of the eight-syllable line must later rhyme with
that of the subsequent six-syllable line and so forth.

Countless beings have fought
Against Man's sins and sought their peace,
But mortal greed won't cease,
Abysmal as the seabeds deep.
Hence, for themselves they keep
The blood-stained spoils they reap and steal.

So few of them may feel
For those whose scars won't heal or fade.
But now, their graves they've made,
And blood's by blood repaid in kind.
Each mortal now shall find
Terror etched in his mind and heart

As heaven's torn apart
By lightning's claws that smart the sky.
Smoke blinds the stars up high;
The stench of death nearby is strong.
Burned piles of corpses on
Charred, blood-soaked soils grow longer still.

A soul-consuming chill
Would haunt the fields and fill the air.
The roars of cannons there

Drown out the mortals' blaring screams.
Nightmarish are the scenes
Where thick dust cloaks the gleams of blades.

Crushed remnants of brigades
Lie scattered in the shades of night
Beneath the Dragon's flight,
Whose rampage paints this sight of Hell,
Where men like squashed flies fell;
Their deaths, though, cannot quell her ire,

Fierce as the raging fire
That burns like her desire to slay
The beasts that took away
Her hatchling. They shall pay with blood!
When she was out for food,
They struck before she could return–

Of which she'd later learn.
She, with her stomach churning, cried
And numbly coiled beside
Her poor kin's blood–long dried–at home.
Her treasures were all gone,
But her eyes were fixed on her child.

There lay her joy and pride,
A headless corpse beside their bed.
Hatred thus seized her head;
By fury urged, she spread her wings.
Destruction she now brings
Upon those rotten things that stole

Away her heart and soul;
Let fiery vengeance fall on them!
The wronged mother's become
The Scourge of Death that, rumbling, burns.
The greed of Mankind earns
Her wrath, and they in turns are shown

The seed of what they've sown:
Their prosperous city's blown to naught.
Amid the dust and rot,
A piercing, sorrow-fraught shriek boomed.
Her tears there are consumed
By the ash of this doomed domain.

Hours of silence reign
Before she once again takes flight.
Man, to her, is a blight–

One she's now sworn to fight and kill,
And she won't stop until
Their kind is purged, then she'll be free

To raise her kin in peace,
To let them grow and seize the skies.
Heaven shakes with her cries,
As she, determined, flies away
Toward where more humans stay—
A new Age of Decay has dawned.

The Last Days of the Flu

Holly Day

We move like dying butterflies against each other
chitinous wings rasping dry in final death throes
like dead leaves pushed along the sidewalk by the wind
like dead scales sloughed off against a rock.

I hear my jagged breath echoing your own feeble one
lungs rattling like an engine running dry but refusing to die
gears almost catching but slipping again and again
if I stay here too long, here, next to you
I might catch it, too.

After an Industrial Accident

Steven Withrow

The Holst Mill closed for good on Christmas Eve,
And the star that led us scattered workers home
Was not a star but Saturn. Ealing Chrome
Would hire on most of us, but to believe
We felt no fear then, severance pay aside,
Was to go too far. Besides that, six had died.

The deaths came all at once, an hour before:
A crew assigned to fix a cooling bed
For I-beam steel. And now the six were dead,
Their bodies reddening the concrete floor.
Alarms—the rollers stopped—we moved to go,
Fleeing the mill to shuffle through the snow.

(The Holst Corp. footage showed an orb of white,
Like a flashbulb burst, and then its negative,
The pupil of a lidless eye. To give
A more precise report, or to say that night
What lit a cosmic flare that killed a crew,
Was more than the local fire chief could do.)

For those who chose to work in furnace heat,
Trained for smelting iron ore perhaps
Or pouring molten slag, crossing the gaps

Between the safe and the strange was no great feat.
Yet nature at its worst, we knew, could not
Produce a form so hideously wrought.

Some parts we later learned or else we dreamed.
Even the ones who'd stood outside the blast
Shunted what we'd witnessed to the past
Till visions overtook us and we screamed.
At the mill again, we watch them turned to flame
By something only exorcists could name.

A Voice in the Night

Geoffrey Reiter

We sent a signal deep into the night,
A puling pulse cast cautiously into
An empty airless ocean, for we knew
(Or thought we knew) that in its fluttering flight
It fain would find a friend. We shone a light
Through dark demesnes to blaze the blue-black queue
Of quasars, nebulae, with all the rue
Of desolation, desperate for the sight
Of one bare blip in answer, just a whisper,
A voice not ours from out the cosmos. But
The night spills only silence, and our prone
Scared souls behold the cold sky, keener, crisper.
And in the deathly dearth of winter, what
Wise words will warm us . . . if we are alone?

Djinn

Christian Dickinson

Upon the barb'rous sands of Araby,
Where burning gales sweep 'cross the barren waste,
A thief upon the wretched hell-scape paced,
Until a great stone edifice did see.

A door, ornate, was carved upon the face,
Which reached unto the apex of the dome;
A tomb of kings, where treasure great found place,
And worship of the Bedouin a home.

The thief, a stone into the darkness cast,
And heard the shatter of an earthen jar.
A cloud of fire rose up from out the tomb,
And did a wrathful giant's form assume:
"You dare entrap me, and my freedom bar!"
One snap—and new dust joined the desert vast.

I Am Beautiful

Ashley Dioses

I'm Heaven sent, you still could say—
From up there I came down.
My gorgeous wings are tarnished gray,
And soot is on my gown.

At last, with Michael we both fought
One desperate final round;
Against or with, it matters not—
Just when I hit the ground.

Blackberries' thorns gave me a prick
As I fell on their vine.
To not be mocked, I played a trick,
Let loose my bitter wine.

Past Michaelmas, if these you try,
Their taste will taint your tongue.
Their poisoned pulp will have you die—
You'll wish that you were hung.

Final Night

DJ Tyrer

When the lights fail
For the final time
And, things long forgotten
Return to the world
Mankind cowers as it did once
Long, long seasons ago
Trapped in a final night

Vampire

Carole Abourjeili

A crowd of demons dressed to thrill
Crawling death
The earth stood still
A lonesome season in disguise
Evil incarnate shall rise
Liquid dreams
"Thus blood shall stain
Let not my death be done in vain"
"Not yet, you shan't walk the un-dead
Nor quench your thirst with the thick red"
And so, he sits with bated breath
Bewitched by the lust of his own death
Not bitten, yet, by the spell of night
Not yet kissed by the sunlight.

A crowd of demons
Hush! Beware!
Let not your hell fall with despair
"Thy blatant lust beware to flaunt
Thy craving passions thus death did haunt"
Liquid dreams in the night they swept
With silent blood craving they crept
Thus, quenched their famine beneath his skin
Bewitched by death, no more. He wept.

***

A crowd of demons
One frightening stare
Beckoning to hell with wild despair
Awakened blood lust in his eyes
His skin, so pale
His fears realised
He sobs, no more, upon his grave
His corpse, thus, treads amongst the brave
He whets his fangs
He craves to bleed
Hush! Here comes his need to feed
Knock! Knock!
He preys right at your door
He flaunts a grin that you adore
The cloak of horror
He pries with sin
Knock! Knock!
Will you invite him in?

Inspired by the mystery game entitled "Haunted House" that I wrote and created for John William.

Time of Day

Jay Hardy

See that woman sitting over there?
Ghost white skin, jet black hair.
She always arrives just after dark.
Sits by herself in the park.
Yes, that's her, under the oak.
Head tilted back. Having a smoke.
I once sat down next to her.
How long ago? I'm not quite sure.
I was much younger at that time.
When saying hello wasn't a crime.
I just inquired in the usual way:
She looked pale. Was she okay?
She assured me that she was fine.
I declined a cigarette. I had mine.
I was a bit startled when she smiled.
Her teeth were long. They looked filed.
Nonetheless, she was good company.
We talked for hours under that tree.
Until she said, "I'm hungry this time of day."
I mumbled some excuse. I didn't stay.
She let me go. I was never sure why.
For whatever reason. I never pry.
I keep my distance. I prefer to wave.
I'm not ready for an early grave.
She waves back. She returns my smile.

But I know they weren't made by file.
Still, I'm drawn to her. Are you not?
Tomorrow, I'll take you to her plot.
I followed her home many years ago.
It's in a cemetery you may know.
Unless you prefer meeting. It's up to you.
She met so many. I've warned a few.
I'll rake my leaves while you decide.
If she's worth knowing. If I lied.

Grindevil

Lori R. Lopez

Was there a moment I could have
turned? A chance to take the other
route—choose another way down
from the top of that steep hill—
along the side of a vacant church
where no choir can sing for they lie
in caskets at the base of the slope,
stacked in the Mortuary without
a Funeral Director.

And birds drop like stones; precursors
of disaster, of doom. But none percuss,
as if I am a memory, lacking firm
substance or shape. I think it is merely
my fate to walk this journey unscathed,
disconnected. So terribly alone.
I cannot glimpse the sunrise ahead,
or feel the blood surge through my
veins, numb and hollow.

I hold my hat in hand, undaunted by
the moon's silver touch, less radiant
than the gold embrace of dawn . . .
footfalls slow, the pace of mourners
in a street procession behind a hearse.
I follow nothing, yet hear the echo

of hoofbeats, my pulse in ears, the swift
heartrate of apprehension, sensing
a presence before me.

I am the last vestige of humankind
in a desolate burg. This wretched
ungodly hellhole that has no name
or mark on a map; constructed of scrap,
fallen timber, the remains of a prior
town that met the same ruin. The only
survivor in the scourge's unhallowed
wake; his path as he circles back
to collect, consume my soul . . .

The one who escaped. I did so
by sitting and listening in the dark.
This time I won't be as lucky.
I can't keep still. Nervous, limbs
trembling. He will discern my steps.
The fiend can hear a blink in a bunker!
The first sign is a crescent smile,
a dangling half-moon grin before
the Devil takes you . . .

With a snatch of claws and the bite
of sly, tickled, beamish teeth. Just that

mirthful gleam until he strikes, that wry
glimmer. Most could not stay quiet.
They're dead now, the lot of them.
I ran, faster than the Dickens.
Then had to return. I had nowhere
to go, just this village where once
I entered the world.

The point from which I must depart.
My treads are a metronome of sorrows,
but I must give the Grindevil his due.
And we will laugh about this . . . racked by
loud belly-gripping guffaws on the other
side. Wind, carry my words to any who
might hear, for this warning is all
that may be left of me when I am gone.
He doesn't care about our cries or tears.

Nor is he a demon we knew before
his arrival. Swooping from the Stars,
some other dimension. A realm empty
as the bucket kicked upon our exit.
Absorbing, draining Essence to fill
the bottomless void of his form.
I suspect he digests it as quickly,

always in need of more. A glutton.
Never pausing to chew.

Fingertips brush cool rough stone,
paint and brick as I descend to greet
a smirking fate, a snickering evil.
We knew the consequences of living,
breathing, tasting each moment.
Helpless we watched them deplete,
flicker away, flutter like ashes in
the breeze. Wondering which
of them were wasted, could have
been wrung more fully, drank
and experienced much deeper . . .
richer . . . better.

This is what we do at the end,
we question and squander time
regretting what we didn't do,
when that no longer matters!
Unless we're unable to see, to hear
or smell what comes. I've had
weeks to prepare, anticipate, accept.
It isn't as if I could pack for a trip,
decide what to bring. Vengeful,

the Grindevil savors my suffering.
Wants me to wait and be afraid.
I won't give him the satisfaction.

I will cling to every last drop
of Life. And then I must strive
to knock that smile right off
his dreadful mug! I don't know
if it's even possible, yet what
have I got to lose?

Perfect World

Ann K. Schwader

No need for change. This planet's perfect now
just as it is: wildfires & hurricanes
no longer seasonal, the monsoon rains
unceasing. Nations never thinking how
they might survive together, pounding plows
back into swords to fillet the remains
of neighbors. Only desiccated plains
reward the victors—something to endow
their children's graves—until the outer dark
approves at last. Forgotten gods we sent
to nightmare wake anew between the stars,
as chaos beckons out of storms that mark
our ravaged atmosphere, & ornament
their perfect world. A world no longer ours.

Bard of Grain and Gourd

K. A. Opperman

For Scott J. Couturier, upon the publication of his collection,
I Awaken in October.

He sings us pumpkin paeans, spectral chants
That prophecy October's chill return.
With druid concentration, he incants
Autumnal spells to help the bonfires burn.

A bard of amber grain and ruddied gourd—
Of grapes that purple on September vines—
His wistful dreams are turned forever toward
October's golden gate, which dimly shines.

Beneath the Ruins of Xul-Kizaak

Wade German

They say the wizard wind that skirls and roams
Around the ruins like some ghost unseen
Was once a demon guard that stood between
The cavern gates to crypts and catacombs;
That still, it wards against all souls who dare
To seek what elder relics might remain
In caves where kings for eons now have lain,
That beasts from myth and legend used as lairs.

The nearest tribes say when the seven moons
Align to bathe the site in greenish rays,
A sect of warlocks gathers at those caves . . .
The wind is weirder then, a voice that croons,
And carries evil shrieks and chants to raise
Ancestral things which crawl from ancient graves.

Marble Fang

Benjamin Blake

The bloodstained banner is unfurled
I refuse to unlearn all I fought for.
So I will invoke the old gods,
Laurel-wreathed and bacchanalian.
To give strength to these etched hands
To execute the necessary slaughter.

There are new lands to conquer
Vineyards and maidens as rewards.
The finest vintage,
The faintest flesh.
On which to feed
In a delicate frenzy.

The words hold power
Ancient and unrivalled,
And will enter through the ears and eyes
And make their inebriating way
Through the labyrinth of vessels and arteries
To finally settle
In the chamber of the heart.

And the city
Shall sigh
Within its
Once-wounded walls.

Love Song of the Lugubrious Gondolier

Manuel Arenas

Good night my little darkling, rest peacefully, sleep tight;
follow the dwindling light, but don't let the vampires bite.
Their mouths besmirched red, though promising life, bear the curse of
   the undead.
Rest easy in your narrow bed, mind not tiny feet, which round the rim
   tread.
Red-hot-skinned *putti*, threshing webbed wings, coriaceous and sooty,
Whose sole, solemn duty is to safe-keep and guard a moribund beauty.
Black vitric stars die when you close your kohl-ed eyes;
their unison cry is doused in your mortal sighs.
Black lustrous locks spread upon the bolster beneath your head;
Their jetty strands thread into the penumbrae your dark dreams shed.
Lest I appear to be remiss, pray, allow me this last good-night kiss
Upon your lips—a moment's bliss!—ere you plunge into the abyss.
Fret not my dying dear, for I shall deftly punt and steer
Your anima from what you fear, as a psychopomp-cum-gondolier,
O'er the vast Phlegethontal streams, the lake of fire that carries and
   breams
Our funereal ferry, past groping teams of bedeviled souls as you lull in
   their screams.

There's a Hole in the Sky

Maxwell I. Gold

There's a hole in the sky with a mouth of darkness prepared to swallow tomorrow, bile and blackness dripped from the slit edges of bleeding lips that knew not laughter; only desiccated sadness and hatred. No one cared to ask where the subversion of the heavens began, firmaments scorched with untruth and faulty visions that marched through the streets praising the gaping wide causeways that bent and blasted stars as if they were dust beneath my feet. *Though what else was to be done when there were holes in the sky?*

Scars never to be healed, cuts to forever bleed and spill the blood of gods and planets through rift and ruin upon the streets below where I'd see the minds of men curdle in rapacious violence, unable to comprehend or come to terms with the merciless doom that poured from the tearful night. One city after the other like brittle paper folded into the crippled agony that was reality with steel and flame as I was the last to know there was a hole in the sky with a mouth of darkness, prepared to swallow tomorrow.

The Countess

John Thomas Allen

Let the funeral draw down the moon;
if wicked she was, at least allow
her a spoiled feast in the tomb.

Complaints abound about her deeds,
her sullen face, teeth of sharp ivory;
stay for a go at bare bones, pig snouts,
her red sea eyes slaughtering lusty louts.

All knowing, all officious, forget and come
together, mount; your jester faced judges
have marked yourselves in judgment, in shout.

Her eyes roll as midnight ore spat
by the Devil! Paralytics calm in loose
surprise, will Countess Elizabeth Bathory
rise in her stained-glass tomb to surprise

her hooded judges in court jester silk,
prelate hypocrites who smear her name.

Rising in eldritch strokes of ashen blood flame!

Among the Dead

Scott J. Couturier

Sitting besided my window one gray
October's day, I saw a ghost go flying by,
insubstantial as fog & mistral-fleet—
feet brushing just above grasses forlorn,
visage pale & lost-looking, forsook by joy,
a cast of melancholy woe:
as a gust it did go, vanishing amid swirling
incarnadine leaves, leaving me to savor sadness
instead of dread, a sweet & subtle sorrow
as one who grieves for a lover's long-lost face
among the dead.

The Role of Monster
I Embrace

Andrew White

I have a taste, a taste for blood
That will not go away
Every night and every day
I feel a lust for human prey.

I live with this hunger, this hunger of mine,
I'm sick until I've fed.
Down my chin a stream of red,
To this craving I am wed.

I love the texture, the texture of skin
When I devour a face.
Though others view it a disgrace
The role of monster I embrace.

Locus Horroris

A Quaternelle

Frank Coffman

There is a place of Dread, of abject Horror,
Recorded only in dark, secret lore,
In grimoires unknown to most—but not to all!
If found, your soul is lost . . . forevermore.

Few seek it, knowing well what may befall
Their spirit if they heed stark Evil's call,
The beck of that place . . . as vile, grim stories tell
In grimoires unknown to most—but not to all.

Beings of Terror dire and Darkness dwell
In that forbidden zone—much worse than Hell!
Yet some have sought that place, a few have obeyed
The beck of That Land . . . as vile, grim stories tell.

Too late they realize they have been betrayed.
Far, far too late the horrid truths pervade
Their senses, their souls bereft of any Hope. . . .
Those who have sought That Land, those few who've obeyed.

The ones condemned there moan and grovel, grope
For any succor. Their world a hideous kaleidoscope.
They slump along the paths of an endless maze,
Their senses, their souls bereft of any Hope.

Though always a thick and foetid miasmic haze
Roils over that place, a bright, infernal blaze
Tended by Demons of that Nether Night
Lights the dim paths along that endless maze.

That awful place holds every abysmal wight
Ever to torment humans in their plight,
And some for whom there is no common name—
All tended by Demons of that Nether Night.

Phrike, the goddess of Fear is its beldame
Deimos, the king of Terror, Your Soul would claim.
They rule a place of Dread, of abject Horror,
A place for which there is no common name.
If found, your soul is lost . . . forevermore.

Iason's Prospicience; or, Solstyce

Manuel Pérez-Campos

I have drawn the clouds at sunset, across the tiered
roofs of accidie's endless houses and dared my heart
to in-glide with the albatross, high over the wrinkled
sea. The sanity-abolishing spirits of the long unremembered
dead I have pacted with and who stretch soughing
through my dreams are already moving this seaside
away from me even though I sense it not: and when
I return, complexioned by a circuit of star-zones beyond
the bowsprit hitherto unwitnessed and cancelled
with a whisper by a hypnagogia-borne witching Medea—
open-robed to taunt—as revenge for being scorned,
none shall recognize me: instead they will say—He
has hauled rope with that inwardness of a demigod
in which certainties are at every turn being dissolved
into long tracts of unknowing by storm-induced
discontinuities from rest and after wayward sail-less mists
long in eternity strolled Thule—which to us remains
a myth—with Thanatos: of ill allure this avid argute
eater of impressions, many-turned and zephyr-fringed.

Illumination

David Barker

Below the windblown sands of Babylon,
We found an ancient torch within a vault
That had not shone since history's grim dawn
When it was dropped by troops in their assault
Upon the citadel of all divine.
And fleeing with it tucked beneath my robe,
I carried home the torch, there to enshrine
Among my horde of lamps from round the globe.

That night, I filled the bowl and lit the wick,
Then specters flared, chased shadows up the walls—
Demonic shapes that turned our poor souls sick
And caused brave men to scatter down the halls.
Since that cursed night my men are not the same.
They've lost their nerve; alas it's me they blame.

Inspired by H. P. Lovecraft's sonnet "VI. The Lamp" in *Fungi From Yuggoth*.

The Whale Road

Dmitri Akers

The captain called for men to stay aback,
As sailors pulled the nets e'er filled with black,
And came unnatural things that bring great chills,
The which are thrown on deck with inky spills,
There, writhing dread, a merman all intact,
Tho' whalers shook with fear at that ol' fact,
As it's contrary to reality . . .
And look! The beast does wish to be so free,
So that ol' captain orders th'abnormal
Thing killed and rendered down for blubber oil:
"To arms, ye dogs, ye boatswains, all," he cries.
His eyes, azure and bright, conceal the lies.
And horrid was the creature's morbid looks,
With baleen body like leviathans from books,
Adam's ol' ribs it hath; half-faced, a man's,
O'er dozen hellish feet its body spans,
Th'abomination lurked from depths unseen,
With no divine design to find nor glean,
Instead, the sailors thought it Davy Jones'
Hierophant, but the truth remained unknown,
And once the butchers went and cut and toiled,
The fatty blubber, rendered down and boiled,
Began to create stenches 'gainst the ship,
The crew didst sicken, growing blue in lip,
'Twas southern winds the which did sweep the deck,

The smell vanished tho' death remained so dreck,
The blowing wind did set the sailors cold,
And then they saw the lapping waters hold
The seabound demons! All became mere knaves,
Who tried e'er hard to fight against the waves,
Tho' all were lulled into the soundless sleep,
As caterwauling sirens chanted deep
Within the swell o' sucking Charybdis,
And when the boat sank, none thought it amiss.

The Last Refuge

James O'Melia

Residing and gently gliding
On the tops of the taller trees,
Old ghosts that know all the slick tricks
Cling like plaque to teeth, to the last
Thing they can on this flawed planet.

Solid branches and leafy niches
Are what they clutch with white knuckles
Holding on for dear life after death
As the winds of climate change
Shake them to their phantom bones.

Perched precariously like balloons,
Subject to drifting up and away,
These departed souls will soon move on
From where they've managed to rest in leaves.
They warily await the chill
Of metaphysical winter.

Let There Be Light

Carl E. Reed

> Only the dead have seen the end of war.
> —Plato

I awake with a start in threatening dark
    nightmare fading like faerie;
heart beating hard as a runaway drum—
    I'm adrenalized, terrified, wary.

Fields of war—long distant now—
    bloom hot & lurid as life
in my dreaming mind—as gun, land mine,
    grenade & combat knife

reap anew their killing tolls—
    I return each night to the fight:
a wraith of Valhalla forever doomed
    to reenact hideous rites.

I reach for my wife, but she isn't there;
    Fran's leapt from the combat bed
to flick a switch & blind with light
    this revenant back from the dead.

The Séance

Ngo Binh Anh Khoa

It was supposed to be a simple day
Where I'd employ some misdirection and
Put on a cogent show where I'd command
Some ghosts to speak and have the gullible pay
My rent. As such, I told my clients to
Sit in a circle with our hands entwined
To start the séance, but I would soon find
A chilling, alien presence passing through
The scented air around us, filling all with dread;
Out of the shadow came harsh grunts and growls
Which rang chaotically; those wretched howls
Toward the end would echo in my head.
I could not comprehend the words It spoke,
But in my mind, I'd see a realm of smoke
Where shriveled figures would collapse and choke.

Now, I'm locked in this padded cell alone,
Believed to have murdered my clients when
I lived whereas they'd met a gruesome end,
Their withered corpses drained of blood. Unknown
Was how they'd died, but still, I had to be
In this madhouse to soothe the public fear,
And few are granted clearance to go near
My cell, which further strains my sanity.
Their wary whispers reach my ears, but more

Than that, I hear the terrible murmurs from
The Thing that joined the séance, which would come
To me each hour, louder than before.
Grotesque sights Its strange words to me reveal,
And as time ticks away, I'd gradually feel
My reason fading, knowing not what's real.

What was at first a jumbled mess of sounds
Now bears significance, which I discern
Through visions of a dark world where things burn,
And humanoid husks fill up the nameless mounds.
Their blood and souls from out their bodies fly
And are absorbed by something in the air—
Made of a billion screaming faces. There,
They'd join that writhing Mass and shrilly cry.
Beneath that Orb of flesh of blood, I find
A lonesome figure wildly singing and
There serving as Its anchor to the land,
Whose face I know well, for I've seen it—mine!
Those haunting scenes play as the murmurs ring
Still in my head, eclipsing everything
Till I, succumbing to It, rise—and sing.

At the Polar Gatefires

Andrew Kolarik

Along the grey pathway, that was etched in dried grass, the thought
    started to prey on me.
I wanted to see it again, just once.
Back there, back in Antarctica, on the roof of the world, the Gateway
    City.
The obsidian arch, five miles high, leaping up to where the stars begin. A
    conglomerate
of bone and iron across the icefields, totems shining on a river of
    mercury.
A nexus, in that wide expanse, of steel and fleshy organics,
a gateway to the stars, I wanted to go there, be with Melanie.

There was a kind of skin, or leathery meniscus, stretched across the arch.
    When it burst,
in a maelstrom of colour and flame, as the wrecking ball hit, I ran, she
    stayed.
A visitation. An intrusion shattered the city, turned the ice to parched
    land, mutable, cursed.
Turned the citizens to croaking, moaning, mewling things, scattered the
    city with holy bones,
alien hardware, weird, high technology. A changing realm, of stretched,
    tortured
membranes and ligaments. I followed the roads, the mass migration.
Or be a crawling, flopping denizen of the place. Leave or be altered.

Perhaps, in time, the land will recover, and ice over the dead city.
At the polar gatefires, there is warmth and comfort, at the roof of the
    world,
in this seething entropy, something of myself will be preserved. It has got
    its claws in me,
it draws me. Will I be improved, or will I transcend, with the
    companions I have made?
As my bones soften, in among this desolate, insane corporeal beauty,
as the buildings groan and shift, as my mind and my memories turns to
    tallow,
with her mystery, her shadow, I will warm my hands here, in the
    Southern Wastes.

Loyal Companion

Steven Withrow

Being a dog of war, a trench-bred cur,
I wake in mud beside my sleeping master
And snap at a rat that crept too close to camp.
The rat is fast, but I am faster.

Then, having breakfasted, I prop my head
Against my master's rifle barrel. Dawn
Gnaws hard at the black bones of night,
And as it breaks, I growl, *Sleep on.*

An hour. And now the company has stirred.
Twelve men, two dogs. I nip my master's shin,
Expecting him to flinch and quickly rouse,
But he's gone stiff, his heart done in.

I wait till someone comes, but who is this?
The stinks of muck and ash confuse my nose.
My master's shape it is, but not his face.
This face is pearly, and it glows.

Being a dog of war, a soldier's mongrel,
I leap up at his call, his voice a boy's,
And leave my filthy bed, my fur, to chase
Him out of smoke and out of noise.

Fuath

Christian Dickinson

In Sutherland, among the Highland Lochs,
Hard by the mosses and the peatlands bare,
A wayward youth did travel with a hare,
Which scraped and scratched inside a wooden box.

All full of spiders was the young boy's mind,
And steeped in naught but blood and cruelty.
The villain did that gentle rabbit bind,
To drown it in a bog upon the lea.

Upon the brink, the foulest of the bogs,
The young boy knelt and opened wide his case.
A stirring in the water brought him near—
A head, o'erspread with pustules, did appear;
Two arms enwrapped in algae grasped his face,
And pulled the knave beneath the chirping frogs.

A Display of Affection

Harris Coverley

Stars
    Spread out
    On the galaxy's edge

A love to be proved
    Between two beings
        Little lesser than gods

The male immortal and his tools:
Forces bending and combined
Stars crushed into stars
    Planets rock and gas crumbled
        Into fleeing solar winds

Strands of star stuff yellow-white
    Hydrogen burning into long lines
Looping to form a simple shape:
    A *heart* for his *sweetheart*

The briefest gift for his beloved

They embrace
    As the monstrosity collapses—
    An angry new nebula
    Devoid of life forevermore

*   *   *

A unique display of affection
And it only cost the universe a mere
    Five technologically-advanced civilisations
    Twelve genuinely sentient species
    And about thirty or so primordial soups
        Which will now never get a chance

In the Ruins

Geoffrey Reiter

Imagine standing on a darkling plain
Stretched out across a distant, dying world
Around a red and bloated sun. Unfurled
Brown clouds roll out above the tangled skein
Of bone-brined dust a stretch where shadows reign.
Upon the plain, you see huge fragments hurled
Of ancient monuments; dry winds have swirled
The lone and level sands like choking rain.

Imagine life among the dusty gusts
That flutters, scuttling underneath the tombs
And toppled towers, testifying death.
This life, amid the tatters and the rusts,
Looks up and sees a gleam between the glooms,
A chasm in the clouds to cleaner breath.

Classic Reprints

The Skeleton Dance: A Ballad

Anonymous

The anthem is chaunting—the priests kneel around
No unlistening ear in the village is found,
The loud-swelling chorus flies upward to heaven,
To the organ's full peal a fresh volume is given—
The day is now waning—declining the sun,
And the Lord's-day bless'd matins are over and done.

A troop of young villagers outward are pressing,
All greeting, and laughing, and joyful caressing.
Young Roger de Tracy and Ralph Boranville,
Robert Wivell was there, and the young Amourduile.
All gay-blooded Normans—in tourney or court
Could none match the youths of fair Rix-à-la-Port.

The moon she shone mildly, the stars twinkled bright,
And flooded the Chapel with silvery light—
The spires and gravestones look'd gay; and the trees
Seem'd tipped with fair splendour, and waved in the breeze;
And out rush'd the band of the villagers gay
As the last anthem-peal was dying away.

"Ho! ho!" cried young Roger, "a night such as this
Is sacred to lovers and kisses and bliss—
What say'st, sweet Sibylla? what, comrades? what, ho!
Shall we creep to our couches demurely and slow?

Let us hail yon fair goddess—ay now, ere we rest—
Let us hail her with revel, with dance, and with jest."

Then loud laugh'd his comrades, and shouted assent,
"Let us to the Green;" but now, as they went,
The holy monk Francis besought them to stay,
"Oh! sin not," he cried, "oh! think on the day—
Oh! think that God hallow'd this day out of seven—
Oh! think that to pleasure six days hath he given!"

"Away with thy priestcraft," cried Roger with scorn,
"We will dance, we will jest, we will revel till morn!
Nay, to punish thy pride, and throw shame on thy face,
Instead of the Green, we will dance in this place!
Over the gravestones and over the dead!"—
"Ay, ay," all his revelling company said.

All but one—and he was the young Amourduile;
The rest of the band could not hear—could not feel.
"Dear Matilda," cried he, "oh! quit, love, this place!"
But she jeer'd at his fears, and laugh'd in his face,
"Go, coward," she said, "go pray if you will,
Give me dance and high revel the sunbeams until."

And now each brave youth has a fair partner led
To dance o'er the gravestones and over the dead;

And loud shouted Roger, and Sibyl laugh'd high,
As over the tombs and the flesh-grass they fly.
And holy St. Francis went mutt'ring away,
"Ay—dance on for ever—forever, for aye!"

Then revell'd they on, and the moon she shone bright,
And still they dance on, as departed the night;
And then fathers and mothers and elders so grey
Pray'd in vain that they'd stop, in vain that they'd stay.
They laugh'd at their fathers, they jeer'd at the grey,
And all went with jokes or profaneness away.

Still they danced—still they danced, but now nothing said!
As they rush'd o'er the gravestones and over the dead.
No laughter's now heard—no revel—nojeer—
They seem'd not to see, or to feel, or to hear!
The maidens look'd pale, and no cheek there was red,
As they flew o'er the gravestones and over the dead.

The morning-blush now had just dappled the sky,
Still o'er the churchyard—ah! fastly they fly!
The villagers gazed on the horrible band,
And speechless—and motionless—spiritless stand.
Some pray—some lament—some weep, and some kneel,
When rush'd from the village the young Amourduile.

"Matilda! Matilda, oh! stop thee," he cried;
"Oh! quit soon this horrible motion, my bride."
She stopp'd not a moment, and nothing she said,
Rut flew o'er the gravestones and over the dead;
And on rush'd the band with the swiftness of light
And whirl'd round and round in the villager's sight.

In young Amourdnile rush'd—the band soon came round.
He flew to Matilda, and caught her fast round.
She was icy—his blood thrill'd—but still he held fast
And on rush'd the horrible company past,
And on swept Matilda—with fright and alarm
He found he clasp'd still but a skeleton-arm!

Then vanish'd the band—though that night every year
Their dance you may see—their shrieks you may hear—
There lash'd by fierce spirits, they sweep on till morn,
Who treated God's day and his servants with scorn.
There the Skeleton Dance may be seen, it is said,
Dance over the tombstones and over the dead.

[From *New Monthly Magazine and Literary Journal* 5 (1 March 1823): 215–16. Thanks to Darrell Schweitzer for passing on the text of this poem.]

Haunted Houses

James F. Morton

Haunted houses, haunted houses! I can see them in my sleep.
Hints of dark, unhallowed orgies make my flesh begin to creep.
Sudden lights at darkened windows, knocking on the floors and walls,
Sounds of wild, unearthly moaning, phantom touches, mystic calls,
Rattling chains and groans of anguish, charnel odors, shrieks of fear,
Rusting gowns and stealthy footfalls, candles dimmed and peril near,
Clashing swords and falling corpses, steps upon the creaking stair,
Chairs upset and toppling tables, thrills of terror everywhere,
Bed by ghostly fingers shaken, bedclothes plucked by unseen hands,
Lamplight suddenly extinguished, as the unknown Will commands,
Words of ghastly import whispered, noises of no mortal source,
Frightful knowledge of the presence of a dire, resistless force,
Faces in the darkened corners, forms beyond all speech uncouth,
Eld unreverend and loathsome, hell-marked childhood, sin-stained youth,
Bullet holes in pallid foreheads, bleeding breasts and throats agape,
Eyes in dreadful frenzy rolling, lips with mow of demon-ape,
Bony hands that slowly, sternly beckon, though no word is said,
Till we needs must rise and follow, at the bidding of the Dead,
While our ghastly leader ever moves with spectral glide before,
Till we gain the place that covers foul or nameless deed of yore;
Ever striving to our vision some grim secret to disclose,
That the task may be accomplished, which shall bring at last repose.
If we win, a soul is ransomed; it we falter, all is lost;
If we fail to read the secret, we must pay the fearful cost.
For the wight who rashly enters, looms the madhouse or the tomb;
Venture not in haunted homes, lest you meet a fearful doom.

[From *Weird Tales* 3, No. 3 (March 1924): 84.]

Reviews

Demonic and Darkling

Leigh Blackmore

WADE GERMAN. *Psalms and Sorceries*. New York: Hippocampus Press, 2022. 118 pp. $15.00 tpb.

Wade German's weird verse has already made its considerably impressive mark in recent years. His first collection, *Dreams from a Black Nebula* (also from Hippocampus Press), appeared in 2014 to wide acclaim. German demonstrated there his mastery of formal verse forms such as the quatrain, sonnet, and the sestina, while also offering work in free verse that gave his macabre imagination a fertile ground for exploring weird conceptions both antique and futuristic.

German continues this approach in his new collection, an earlier version of which was published by Mount Abraxas Press as *Ladies of the Everlasting Lichen and Other Relics*. Various of the poems here gathered have appeared in a wide variety of journals, and one in an anthology.

German divides his psalms and sorceries into three thematic groupings: "Nightscapes" (18 poems), "Prophecies & Dooms" (15 poems), and "The Monstrous Voice" (3 poems). *Children of Hypnos*, 36 pages long, is an epic poetic drama forming a concluding section all on its own. Many weird poets cannot help but pay tribute through their work to bygone elder "gods" of the genre, and German is no exception; yet in poems such as "Alastor" and "The Ghosts of Hyperborea," which might well be read as tributes to the style and thematic content of a Clark Ashton Smith, German sings in his own clear, true voice. From "Alastor":

> The spirit but a sourceless shadow seems
> Amid mirages on the sighing sands—

Flitting to caves and dark colossal tombs,
Searching for some unknown among those gloom
And silences that speak of other lands,
Of alien worlds that ancient dead men dream.

That final line tellingly combines the cosmic with the funereal, climaxing in a memorable image of dreams dreamt *by the dead*. From "The Ghosts of Hyperborea":

The spirits here were giants in their day—
Great conquerors, whose names were raised in chants
By evil slaves and holy hierophants . . .
But of their chronicles, now none can say.
The bitter, boreal winds that ever gust
Have long-since blown their epitaphs to dust.

German's final line here packs an impact even without his resorting to the oft-seen terminal exclamation mark, and if the image is redolent of Ashton Smith, then let us not complain, but rejoice that German honors one of his poetic mentors thus. The spirit of Klarkash-Ton never seems far from these weird verses, with their frequent references to cosmic matters of time and space, but German wisely refrains from patterning his work too closely upon Smith's own phraseology and vocabulary, even while honoring his far-reaching cosmic themes.

"Ecclesiastical Triptych," consisting of the linked poems "Relics," "Black Robes," and "Ladies of the Everlasting Lichen," is a macabre masterpiece in miniature that deserves to be read again and again. Both conceptually and in execution it is nearly faultless, save the mildly uncomfortable rhyme of "myrrh" and "pure" in stanza 2 of "Relics." I would not wish to meet those Ladies of the Lichen; those "bridesmaids of oblivion" with their "blank wide eyes of milky white" are a truly ghastly trio. German also delights with his use of language here; the adjective "mausolean" is one I had never previously encountered, and is truly well chosen in its present context.

There seems a tip of the hat to Lovecraftian style and thematics in the final couplet of "The Shrine": "And he and all his acolytes were burned / For knowing things not meant for human minds." Other poems in the "Nightscapes" section deal effectively with the ghoulish side of Druidry, witchcraft, demons, ghouls, and the Old Gods.

"Cernunnos" would make a fine chant to be howled in unison by a witchcraft circle in its sacred space while invoking the Horned God . . . And any poet who uses the lovely and rather obscure word "silentious" ("Rune") may, in my opinion, be forgiven the odd small lapse (the rhyme of "knees" and "appeased" in "Druidry").

In the second section, "Prophecies and Dooms," German pays tribute to Robert W. Chambers via a diptych of verses, "Two Songs from *The King in Yellow*," and to the modern master of the macabre, W. H. Pugmire, in "The Tomb of Wilum Hopfrog Pugmire." Fabled biblical giants feature in "Fields of the Nephilim." Bracing nihilism and loss of conventional religious faith are tellingly deployed in the lengthy poem "Lore," which ranges from evocations of lost Mu and Atlantis to "demonic beings from the stars / Who traveled through the gulfs of time and space / From evil planets that no longer are." A similarly pungent nihilism infests "Methuselah." Its concluding lines (comparable in intensity to some of Richard L. Tierney's bitterest poetic sentiments about the pitiful uselessness of humanity) can only be quoted:

> *The human race should not have been . . .*
>
> Lord, how I've come to hate them all,
> The symptom of the universe!
> Heaven, I pray you hear my call
> And heed my prayer, a parting curse:
> That God on them a deluge sends,
> That human filth from Earth is cleansed.

In fact, this poem is less a specimen of nihilistic philosophy than one of anti-natalism, the philosophy espoused by such modern philosophers as David Benatar and influential (along with Emil Cioran and other pessimists) upon, most prominently in the weird field, Thomas Ligotti.

"Beddoes: Marginalia in a Cadaveric Atlas" nods to the graveyard poet Thomas Lovell Beddoes, while creating a uniquely "Germanic" vision of grave-lore not soon to be forgotten. "Philomathes and Epistemon" is a dialogue in the Grecian philosophical sense, written in blank verse, with each speaker—each a spirit resurrected by a necromancer—taking turns to discuss the fate of their souls, the plight in which they find themselves (a cycle of endless return), and the dark enchantments which have brought all this about. An extraordinary piece, which in certain aspects may be comparable in its imagery to some of George Sterling's best lines, for instance, this startling image: "A blood red moon is glowing like the eye / Of blinded Cyclops . . ." Save for some uncertain scansion in some of the final lines, one would be tempted to praise it as one of the finest (and blackest) of weird poems this reviewer has had the pleasure and privilege of reading. Nor does German hesitate to utilize classical references that may escape the modern reader who is not as familiar with the Bible and with the Western canon as is German himself—as in line 23 of this dialogue with its reference to "the error of the Sadducees." (For those who are unsure what this error was, the Sadducees of Jesus' time did not believe in resurrection, angels, and spirits, even though all are addressed in the Old Testament.)

Section 3, "The Monstrous Voice," delves even more deeply into classical myth for its inspiration. "Scylla and Charybdis" is another well-constructed dialogue. If its form recalls similar prose poems by Poe and C. A. Smith, then once again, so much the better. It will be recalled that Scylla and Charybdis were monsters from Greek mythology thought to inhabit the Straits of Messina, the narrow sea between Sicily and the Italian mainland. Preying on passing mariners, Scylla was a monstrous creature with six heads and twelve feet, while Charybdis, living on the opposite side of the straits, was another monster who, over time, was transformed in the imagination of the ancients into a more rational but no less lethal whirlpool. Odysseus famously had to negotiate a passage through their deadly clutches in Homer's *Odyssey*. (It might have been kind to the less classically inclined reader to provide an elucidatory footnote to this effect.)

The volume concludes with the epic poem *Children of Hypnos*, which is, in fact, a play in poetic form (known as a verse drama). This work was first published (as acknowledged in the text) by Raphus Press— apparently, from my research, a publisher in Sao Paulo—as part of a limited edition titled *Apparitions*.

Verse drama goes back as far as the ancient Greeks, and in fact German's verse drama here features Grecian characters. It displays his knowledge of Greek and Roman classics ranging from the *Orphic Hymns* to Lucan's *Pharsalia*. While verse drama was popular among such earlier writers as Shakespeare, Ben Jonson, and John Fletcher, and later Goethe and the early Henrik Ibsen, there is scarcely a verse drama to be found in modern times, with the exception of such works as George Sterling's *Lilith* and *Rosamund*, Clark Ashton Smith's *The Dead Will Cuckold You*, and *La Beet* by David Hirson, which recasts Molière as verse drama. Thus German's epic here is particularly ambitious and unusual.

Children of Hypnos is mainly written, like the plays of Shakespeare, in iambic pentameter; but there are some rhyming sections of verse, such as the evocation of Hecate by Erichtho. This work is another extraordinary if challenging piece that amply demonstrates both German's deep absorption of classical influences and his capable hand in turning such influences to use in his poetic work. While the reader will need to grapple with what is likely a largely unfamiliar form today, this effort will be amply repaid. German's muse is demonic, despairing, delicious, and darkling by turns.

It only remains to write that *Psalms and Sorceries* is a glittering incunabulum of basalt upon which the poet has inscribed dark runes of magic that will thrust the reader into exquisitely shadowy realms of darkness, human folly, and cosmic terror. What more could one possibly ask from such a collection?

No Happily-Ever-After

Katherine Kerestman

REBECCA BUCHANAN. *Not a Princess, But (Yes) There Was a Pea, and Other Fairy Tales to Foment.* Salem, OR: Jackanapes Press, 2022. 164 pp. $15.99 tpb.

"Beware the Goose Mother," this collection of fairy tale poems begins, for Rebecca Buchanan tells tales of "angry daughters," "mad wives," and "stolen children." I must admit that I came to this volume warily, weary of diatribe and moral exposition, which have in recent times taken the place of meaningful dialogue and reasonable debate in all things contentious. For the most part, Buchanan has avoided this kind of overt proselytization, but at times her fairy tales degenerate into fables and parables illustrative of morals. Her poetry sparkles when it preserves the occult realms of enchanted forests and palaces, princesses and frog-princes—as well as the dark sorcery that permeates fairy tales. During a series of wolf attacks, for instance, the Fairy Godmother is quoted as saying, "My thoughts and prayers are with the princesses and their father during this difficult time. Perhaps they should be locked up for their own safety." Cinderella is a bride who is burnt when the short honeymoon is over, at midnight.

Fairy tales generally describe social ills—such as the misogyny, homophobia, and poverty that are the major threads of Buchanan's tales—acted out by fantastic characters in make-believe places. Traditional fairy tales also generally evince a longing for a better place, but they avoid prescribing behaviors for achieving that state: they simply illustrate the disparities between the imaginary realm of happily ever after and the morbid real world of human society in a cosmos devoid of reason and justice. Bad things happen without provocation and without redress in the Brothers Grimm stories. People are willfully and inexplicably unfeeling, exploitative, and cruel.

Buchanan's poetry is skillful, her imagery inspired. She is much more optimistic than the Grimms: her work resembles the fairy tales of the Victorians—such as were written by Kenneth Graham and John Ruskin—which were designed to inculcate goodness in the impressionable reader, rather than to describe the black and soulless moral void that characterizes the universe of the Brothers Grimm. Sometimes the homily is restrained, allowing the dark fantasy to glitter in all its wickedness, as in "Matches," a poem about the horrors of living in a world forever at war with itself; but sometimes the lesson is rather too blatant, as in the Puss in Boots poem, which is a lesson in the evils of telling people what they want to hear in order to ascend the societal ladder.

The world, alas, is full of Becky Sharpes who are not in the least interested in learning right ways of living, but who prosper at others' expense and thrive upon others' misery. The greatest horror in life is the fact that there is no happily-ever-after—not in the Brothers Grimm and not in the real world. Traditional fairy tales offer the escapism of magical realms in crystal palaces, under the sea, and in the skies; but they do not suggest that these realms are attainable by ordinary mortals. Buchanan's moral optimism, I fear, is the more make-believe of the two attitudes.

October's Law of Diminishing Returns

Steven Withrow

SCOTT J. COUTURIER. *I Awaken in October: Poems of Folk Horror and Halloween*. Salem, OR: Jackanapes Press. 2022. 150 pp. $14.99 tpb.

Had Scott J. Couturier's first volume of poems, *I Awaken in October*, been a slim and modest book of 50 pages and 30 poems, I would have read it once through and then gladly revisited the seven or eight strongest poems, focusing my review on their rhythmic energy and their many felicitous moments.

But instead, what we have is a 150-page "cornucopia" (so says the back cover) of 60 poems complete with several blurbs, a foreword, an introduction, five section breaks, and 20 illustrations. Publisher/designer/illustrator Dan Sauer clearly took pains to make this a memorable and praiseworthy package. His visual work is impressive, both bold and balanced, from front to back.

The trouble is, this book as an object, at its current length, would be a better fit for an anthology of time-tested pieces than for a solo writer's incipient efforts. Simply put, *I Awaken in October* promises too much and delivers too little. (This is, I should say, hardly a problem isolated to Mr. Couturier's book; it is a central dilemma of twenty-first-century poetry: too much for too little, too little for too much.)

Here, the best poems are buried among weaker entries that sometimes seem like overlong drafts of stronger poems and are rife with redundancies and other missteps. Inspired moments appear often, but isolated moments do not make powerful poems, and I found myself skimming over stanzas or full pages.

Let's try to separate the package from the poems, however, and see what still sings.

The first poem, for instance—"The Gods Came in Autumn"—has one of the book's finest titles and also a well-timed movement from line to line and a careful compression that most of the other poems lack. The images are sharp and specific, and there is a minimum of what I call "faux Poe" in its diction and syntax.

Here are three lines that show off a bit of Mr. Couturier's ability to create unique speech patterns that do not feel false or forced or needlessly repetitive as so much else in the collection unfortunately does:

> The Gods' laughter was crisp &
> sharp as a poniard's killing point:
> in their mirthful wake crept cold.

A few pages later, for aural/oral enjoyment he gives us the 16-line quasi-sonnet "The Pumpkin Sprite." The opening (with its nod to Keats's great ode) reads:

> Pumpkin sprite alighting from gourd to gourd:
> beneath Autumn's amethyst moon grown huge
> she plumpens up pulp & swells seeds in horde,
> subtle spirit of season's subterfuge.

Certain stanzas have a mesmeric power on their own, despite their too-familiar archaisms and metrical inconsistencies, like this one from "Daisies":

> Daisies deign their benign vigil to maintain
> 'till Autumn unwinds its funereal train:
> then wither!, awaiting Spring's succulent rain
> & new thralls to renew old worship again,
> hierophantic plant in mysterium crowned.

And this curious one from "Green Fever" that transcends the poem to which it belongs:

> The growth is spreading.
> In his brain blades of green

> sprout from gray matter,
> piercing a pate laved
> in verdurous sweat-sheen.

In later sections, "Planting Instructions, "Azazel-Pomps," and "Algol's Lamp" should be read in their entirety to appreciate their classic weirdness. The writer is *thinking* in poems like these, not merely riffing on a theme in vague words—and, strange as they are, they stay in the mind.

Later in the book are a handful of solidly wrought narrative poems that remind me of the work of Frank Coffman. My three favorites are "Old Black Shuck," "The Nachzehrer," and "When Black Tom Came." The closing stanza of "The Nachzehrer" provides a particularly chilling resolution:

> Through her jaw a shaft of ashwood driven,
> head clean from her shoulders then rudely cleft.
> Again she claims what life is her given:
> all her kindred fall dead, of blood bereft.
> By livid lightning heaven is riven.

The final part of the book, "A Crown of Seasons," is the weakest of the group, with few new tones or imaginative leaps, and it points back to the quantity-versus-quality problem of the project as a whole.

That said, while *I Awaken in October* might be stretched skeletally thin in terms of substance at 150 pages, it still has more to recommend it than so much of what I've been skimming in poetry these days, and I can't help but admire the ambition of both writer and artist/publisher for making it available to us.

Notes on Contributors

Carole Abourjeili lives in Australia, with her daughter, Rumi. Having attended a French school in Lebanon, Carole is fluent in Arabic, French, and English. She won her first poetry prize in a university competition for her poem "Awakening," later published in *Spectral Realms* 1. "I fell in love with poetry at the age of nine after seeing my grade 4 teacher obsess with the literature and poetry of the great Nizar Qubani."

Dmitri Akers is a writer and poet living on Kaurna land (Adelaide, South Australia). His creative work has appeared in *La Piccioletta Barca* and *So It Goes*; his nonfiction has appeared in the *Modernist Review* and on the Undergraduate Library (as he was Highly Commended by the Global Undergraduate Awards in 2020).

John Thomas Allen's favorite poets are all spooky, whether or not they fit into so-called "genre poetry." There has to be something strange about the stuff to get him interested. New York is one of the great homes of "surreal poetry," and he is now reading Eric Basso's *Catafalques*, hoping his chapbook *Cemetery Tour* finds a publisher. (They really do that—give tours for cemeteries.)

James Arthur Anderson is a retired English professor who now teaches part-time at East Georgia State College. His speculative poetry has appeared in *Star*Line*, *Scifaikuest*, *Ilumen*, and *Asimov's Science Fiction*. He has also published several critical studies, including *Out of the Shadows: A Structuralist Approach to Understanding the Fiction of H. P. Lovecraft*, *Excavating Stephen King*, and *The Linguistics of Stephen King*. He lives in Garfield, Georgia, with his wife Lynn.

Manuel Arenas resides in Phoenix, Arizona, where he writes his Gothic fantasies and dark ditties sheltered behind heavy curtains, as he shuns the oppressive orb that glares down on him from the cloudless, dust filled desert sky. His work has appeared in various genre publications, most notably in the poetry journal *Spectral Realms*.

David Barker has been writing supernatural fiction and poetry since the mid-1980s. In collaboration with the late W. H. Pugmire, he wrote three books of Lovecraftian fiction: *The Revenant of Rebecca Pascal* (2014), *In the Gulfs of Dream and Other Lovecraftian Tales* (2015), and *Witches in Dreamland*, (2018), all three of which will be published in German-language editions. David's work has appeared in many magazines and anthologies including *Fungi, Cyäegha, Weird Fiction Review, The Audient Void, Nightmare's Realm, Forbidden Knowledge, Spectral Realms, The Art Mephitic,* and *A Walk in a Darker Wood.* David's collection of horror stories *Her Wan Embrace* will be published in 2022. He lives in Oregon with his wife, Judy.

Leigh Blackmore's horror fiction has appeared in more than sixty magazines from *Avatar* to *Strange Detective Stories.* He has reviewed for journals including *Lovecraft Annual, Shoggoth, Skinned Alive,* and *Dead Reckonings.* His critical essays appear in volumes including Benjamin Szumskyj's *The Man Who Collected Psychos: Critical Essays on Robert Bloch,* Gary William Crawford's *Ramsey Campbell: Critical Essays on the Modern Master of Horror,* Danel Olson's *21st Century Gothic,* and elsewhere. New weird verse has appeared in *Penumbra* and other journals.

Benjamin Blake is the author of the novel *The Devil's Children* and the poetry collections *Standing on the Threshold of Madness, Southpaw Nights* (poetry and prose), *All the Feral Dogs of Los Angeles* (with Cole Bauer), *Dime Store Poetry,* and *Tenebrae in Aeternum* (published by Hippocampus Press). He resides in Cuernavaca, Mexico.

Adam Bolivar is a poet of dark fantasy, a weird fiction writer, and a playwright for marionettes with a particular interest in balladry, alliterative verse, and "Jack" tales. He is the author of *The Lay of Old Hex* (Hippocampus Press, 2017), *The Ettinfell of Beacon Hill* (Jackanapes Press, 2021), *Ballads for the Witching Hour* (Hippocampus Press 2022), and the forthcoming *A Wheel of Ravens* (Jackanapes Press, 2023). A native of Boston, Massachusetts, he now resides in Portland, Oregon.

William Clunie is an American poet living in Berlin. His work has appeared in *Dreams and Nightmares, Star*Line,* and as a collection from Demain Publishing, *Laws of Discord.* He would like to think his primary influences are Shakespeare, Milton, and Poe. He is married to a German woman named Sandra. They are quite happy together.

Frank Coffman is a retired professor of college English and creative writing. He has published speculative poetry, fiction, and scholarly essays in a variety of magazines and anthologies. His poetic magnum opus, *The Coven's Hornbook and Other Poems* (January 2019), has been followed by his rendition into English verse of 327 quatrains in his collection *Khayyám's Rubáiyát* (May 2019). Both books were published by Bold Venture Press.

Scott J. Couturier is a Rhysling Award–nominated poet and prose writer of the weird, liminal, and darkly fantastic. His work has appeared in numerous venues, including *The Audient Void, Spectral Realms, Space & Time, Cosmic Horror Monthly,* and *Weirdbook*; his collection of weird fiction, *The Box,* is available from Hybrid Sequence Media, while his collection of autumnal and folk horror verse, *I Awaken In October,* is available from Jackanapes Press.

Along with previously in *Spectral Realms,* **Harris Coverley** has verse published or forthcoming in *Polu Texni, California Quarterly, Star*Line, Scifaikuest, Tales from the Moonlit Path, The Five-Two: Crime Poetry Weekly, View From Atlantis, Danse Macabre, Once Upon A Crocodile,* and many others. A past Rhysling Award nominee and member of the Weird Poets Society, he lives in Manchester, England.

Christian Dickinson is a native of Jacksonville, Florida, where he attended the University of North Florida for English Education. After teaching three years in Duval County, he was accepted to the Master's Program at Florida State, and then to a Doctoral at Baylor University. He is currently working on a book of beast-poems, three of which are featured in the current issue.

Steve Dilks is an English writer working in the new pulp field. He has written SF, fantasy, and horror for Pulp Hero Press, Wildside Press, Literary Rebel LLC, and Parallel Universe Publications. Under his own Carnelian Press banner, he is the author of two collections: *Gunthar–Warrior of the Lost World* and *Black Dust and Other Stories*. His poem in this issue marks his debut appearance in *Spectral Realms*.

Ashley Dioses is a writer of dark poetry and fiction from southern California. Her debut collection of dark traditional poetry, *Diary of a Sorceress*, was published in 2017 by Hippocampus Press. Her second poetry collection of early works, *The Withering*, was published by Jackanapes Press in 2020.

Joshua Gage is an ornery curmudgeon from Cleveland. His newest chapbook, *blips on a screen*, is available on Cuttlefish Books. He is a graduate of the Low Residency MFA Program in Creative Writing at Naropa University. He has a penchant for Pendleton shirts, Ethiopian coffee, and any poem strong enough to yank the breath out of his lungs.

Adele Gardner's poetry collection *Halloween Hearts* is available from Jackanapes Press. With poems and stories in *Analog, Clarkesworld, Strange Horizons, Daily Science Fiction*, and more, Adele curated the 2019 SFPA Halloween Poetry Reading and serves as literary executor for father, mentor, and namesake Delbert R. Gardner.

Wade German is the author of *Dreams from a Black Nebula* (Hippocampus Press, 2014). His poetry has been nominated for the Pushcart, Rhysling, and Elgin Awards, and has received numerous honorable mentions in Ellen Datlow's *Best Horror of the Year* anthologies.

Maxwell I. Gold is an author of weird fiction and dark fantasy. His work has been published in *Spectral Realms, The Audient Void, Hinnom Magazine*, and elsewhere. His short story "A Credible Fear" will be published in the literary journal *The Offbeat* from Michigan State University's Department of Creative Writing and Rhetoric. He studied philosophy and political science at the University of Toledo and is an active member of the Horror Writers Association.

Amelia Gorman lives in Eureka, California, where she spends her free time exploring the tide pools and redwoods with her dogs and foster dogs. Her fiction has appeared in *Nightscript* 6 and *Cellar Door* from Dark Peninsula Press. You can read some of her recent poetry in *New Feathers, Vastarien*, and *Penumbric*. Her first chapbook, the Elgin-winning *Field Guide to Invasive Species of Minnesota*, is available from Interstellar Flight Press.

Jay Hardy is an artist, editor, and poet from knee deep in the heart of Louisiana's Cajun Country. He is a lifelong fan of "The Alphabet Boys": HPL, REH, ERB, and CAS. His poetry is either weirdly humorous or humorously weird. His poems have appeared in *Ellery Queen's Mystery Magazine* and the *Hyborian Gazette*. His self-published poetry collections include *Always Eleven: Poems Inspired by* Stranger Things, *My Mommy Hates Halloween, Living Longmire, Cats of Cairo,* and *The Paranoid Pirate.*

Chad Hensley is a Bram Stoker Award–nominated author. His most recent book of poetry, *Embrace the Hideous Immaculate,* was published by Raw Dog Screaming Press. His most recent fiction appearance is in the *Weirdbook Annual: Zombies!* issue. His nonfiction has appeared in the magazines *Rue Morgue, Juxtapoz, Terrorizer, Spin, Hustler,* and most recently in *Weird Fiction Review* #11 featuring his in-depth article on Cadabra Records. Look for more his poetry in future issues of *Weirdbook* and online in the Science Fiction Poetry Association's quarterly online journal *Eye to the Telescope* #42: "The Sea."

Ron L. Johnson II has received honorable mention from *Photographer Forum Magazine* and has been published in *Best of College Photography Annual* and *St. Charles Suburban Journal.* Since digitalization has put film on the endangered list, he writes now with words instead of light. He will have an article of criticism published in the 2023 issue of the *Lovecraft Annual.* Ron's writings are influenced by science, art, fantasy, and the macabre.

Hailing from Croydon, **Andrew Kolarik** spent ten years writing post-punk lyrics for live performance in London and Cardiff. He has written poetry, short fiction, and film criticism appearing or forthcoming in *Utopia Science Fiction Magazine, Down in the Dirt, Carillon, Pulp Metal Magazine, Supernatural Tales, Eunoia Review, Horla,* and *Film International.*

David C. Kopaska-Merkel won the 2006 Rhysling award (long poem, written with Kendall Evans), edits *Dreams & Nightmares* magazine (since 1986), has edited *Star*Line,* an issue of *Eye to the Telescope,* and several Rhysling anthologies, has served as SFPA president, and is an SFPA Grandmaster. His poems have been published in *Asimov's, Strange*

Horizons, and more than 200 other venues. *Some Disassembly Required*, a collection of dark poetry, was published this year.

Lori R. Lopez is a quirky author, illustrator, poet, and songwriter. Her Gothic-toned and extensive poetry collection *Darkverse: The Shadow Hours* was nominated for the 2018 Elgin Award. Individual poems have been nominated for the Rhysling Award. Lori's stories and verse appear in numerous publications. Other titles include the *Mister Snark* series, *Leery Lane*, *Odds & Ends*, and *An Ill Wind Blows*.

D. L. Myers is a dark poet from the Pacific Northwest. His work has appeared in *Spectral Realms*, *Eye to the Telescope*, *The Audient Void*, *Black Wings VI*, *The Rhysling Anthology*, *Test Patterns*, and *A Walk in a Darker Wood*. His first collection, *Oracles from the Black Pool*, was published by Hippocampus Press in 2019.

Ngo Binh Anh Khoa is a teacher of English in Ho Chi Minh City, Vietnam. In his free time, he enjoys daydreaming, reading, and occasionally writing poetry for personal entertainment. His speculative poems have appeared in NewMyths.com, *Heroic Fantasy Quarterly*, *The Audient Void*, and other venues.

James O'Melia is a retired mailman and granddad residing in a western suburb of Philadelphia where he enjoys writing haiku, playing chess, and rooting for the Eagles and Phillies. His poems have recently appeared in *Spectral Realms*, *Dreams and Nightmares*, and *Scifaikuest*.

K. A. Opperman is a poet with a predilection for the strange, the Gothic, and the grotesque, continuing the macabre and fantastical tradition of such luminaries as Poe, Clark Ashton Smith, and H. P. Lovecraft. He has published four poetry collections to date: *The Crimson Tome*, *Past the Glad and Sunlit Season*, *October Ghosts and Autumn Dreams*, and *The Laughter of Ghouls*.

Manuel Pérez-Campos's poetry has appeared previously in *Spectral Realms* and *Weird Fiction Review*. A collection of his poetry in the key of the weird is in progress; so is a collection of ground-breaking essays on H. P. Lovecraft. He lives in Bayamón, Puerto Rico.

Carl E. Reed is employed as the showroom manager for a window, siding, and door company just outside Chicago. Former jobs include U.S. marine, long-haul trucker, improvisational actor, cab driver, security guard, bus driver, door-to-door encyclopedia salesman, construction worker, and art show MC. His poetry has been published in the *Iconoclast* and *Spectral Realms*; short stories in *Black Gate* and *newWitch* magazines. His first collection of fiction, *Dark Matter*, is forthcoming from Hippocampus Press.

Geoffrey Reiter is Associate Professor and Coordinator of Literature at Lancaster Bible College. He is also an Associate Editor at the website *Christ and Pop Culture*, where he frequently writes about weird horror and dark fantasy. As a scholar of weird fiction, Reiter has published academic articles on such authors as Arthur Machen, Bram Stoker, Clark Ashton Smith, and William Peter Blatty. His poetry has previously appeared in *Spectral Realms* and *Star*Line*, and his fiction has appeared in *Penumbra* and *The Mythic Circle*.

Silvatiicus Riddle is a dark fantasy and speculative fiction writer living on the borderlands of New York City with a menagerie of cats, a hoard of books, and all his imaginary friends. He has recently been published by *Abyss & Apex, Enchanted Living Magazine, Liquid Imagination,* and *The Quarter(ly)*.

Ann K. Schwader lives and writes in Colorado. Her newest collection, *Unquiet Stars*, is now out from Weird House Press. Two of her earlier collections, *Wild Hunt of the Stars* (Sam's Dot, 2010) and *Dark Energies* (P'rea Press, 2015), were Bram Stoker Award Finalists. In 2018, she received the Science Fiction & Fantasy Poetry Association's Grand Master award. She is also a two-time Rhysling Award winner.

A career retrospective of **Darrell Schweitzer**'s short fiction was published by PS Publishing in two volumes in 2020. A veritable flood of Schweitzeriana is soon to follow from various publishers in the next year or so, including a new Lovecraftian anthology, *Shadows out of Time* (PS), *The Best of Weird Tales: The 1920s* (Centipede Press), *The Best of Weird Tales 1924* (with John Betancourt, Wildside Press), a weird poetry collection, *Dancing Before Azathoth*, a new story collection, *The Children of*

Chorazin (Hippocampus), and two further volumes of author interviews (Wildside). He was co-editor of *Weird Tales* between 1988 and 2007.

DJ Tyrer is the person behind Atlantean Publishing and has been published in *The Rhysling Anthology*, issues of *Cyäegha*, *The Horrorzine*, *Scifaikuest*, *Sirens Call*, *Star*Line*, *Tigershark*, and *The Yellow Zine*. The e-chapbook *One Vision* is available from Tigershark Publishing. *SuperTrump* and *A Wuhan Whodunnit* are available for download from Atlantean Publishing.

M. F. Webb's poetry has appeared in previous issues of *Spectral Realms* and her fiction has been published in *Latchkey Tales*. She resides in a Victorian seaport town not too far from Seattle with her husband and their five adult cats plus one pandemic kitten.

Andrew White is a contemplative, occasionally creative person living in the mountains of North Carolina. He is inspired by mythology, mysticism, and all things Gothic/Lovecraftian. Andrew loves nature, his family, and his books. He tries not to take himself too seriously. *The Voice of Midnight and Other Poems* (digital copy) is available at no cost. Send an email to ADWhite138@gmail.com with the subject line Midnight to receive a copy.

Steven Withrow's poems appear in *Spectral Realms*, *Asimov's Science Fiction*, and *Dreams & Nightmares*. His poem "The Sun Ships," from an Elgin Award–nominated collection of the same title, was nominated for a 2016 Rhysling Award from the Science Fiction & Fantasy Poetry Association. His most recent solo collection is *The Bedlam Philharmonic*. His collection with Frank Coffman, *The Exorcised Lyric*, contains "Toward Solstice Station," a nominee for the 2022 Rhysling Award. He lives on Cape Cod.

Jordan Zuniga is an emerging Christian creative writer who actively writes and promotes on Instagram @cccreativewriter and on vocal.media as Jordan Zuniga. He enjoys writing high fantasy (sometimes a little dark for some Christian audiences) and speculative fiction. He has appearances with *Spectral Realms*, *Christiandevotions.us*, *Poetry Coloring Book: Halloween Edition*, and *Literary Yard* magazine.

www.ingramcontent.com/pod-product-compliance
Lightning Source LLC
Chambersburg PA
CBHW060803050426
42449CB00008B/1513